KV-704-678

START
HERE

C.S.

*When all else fails,
Read the instructions*

Jim

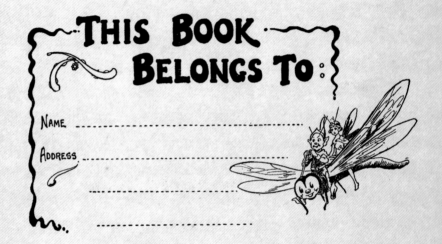

THIS BOOK BELONGS TO:

NAME ....

ADDRESS ....

....

....

*All characters in this book are fictional and **any**
resemblance to persons living or dead is purely
coincidental.*

423393

FANTASY BOOK LIBRARY

18 SOUTHAMPTON ROW, W.C.1.

Telephone: CHAncery 8669

D88	21-3 55	2/-
30 MAR WN		
-9 APR SN		
	PH2	
-2 MAY 1057		
28 JUN C89		
JUL C96		
AUG I21		
20 AUG H93		
3- SEP C6D2		
SEP M18		
29 OCT B88		
3 DEC B93		
25 FEB D98		

WITHDRAWN

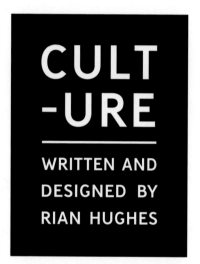

CULT-URE

WRITTEN AND DESIGNED BY RIAN HUGHES

ERRATA

Page 60
Social cues are culturally specific, and so may
not be universally understood.
Maybe s/he likes you, maybe s/he doesn't.

FIELL

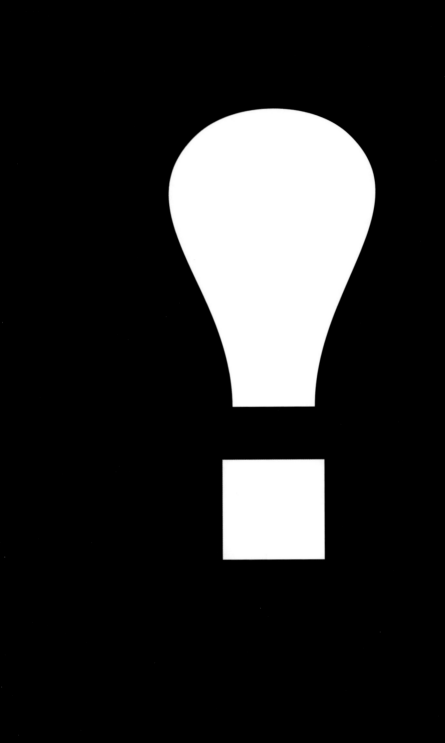

CULT
-URE

"Culture is roughly anything we do and the monkeys don't."
— Lord Raglan

Culture is your local consensus reality; your clothing and cuisine, the music you listen to, the books you read, the films you see; your values, ideas, beliefs and prejudices.

Culture, unlike eye colour or race, is not a compulsory genetic accident of birth, but an *optional intellectual position.*

And unlike your race, your culture is in a vibrant daily state of flux. Your culture is not your parent's culture, nor will it be your children's.

Culture here is different from culture there. Culture now is different from culture then.

Culture evolves – particular cultural ideas can spread rapidly, while others atrophy or are wiped out. Some aspects of culture are fleeting and transient, while other strains are carefully nurtured and survive unchanged for generations.

Today culture has a powerful new vector – *the internet* – and ideas are spreading further and faster than ever before. This new delivery system is unique because despite efforts at regulation it is generally unmediated, democratic, and *two-way* – anyone with a camera and a keyboard can potentially speak to the world.

"We're going to have a new global conversation."
— Jimmy Wales, founder, Wikipedia

So what exactly are we saying to each other?

What ideas are we sharing? What effects are they having?

Who do we think we are and who do we want to be?

These questions are articulated through *culture* . . . and are the very questions *cults* purport to have answers for.

Ideas germinate in culture.

FOREWORD OR BACKWARD

This book is best read in the traditional manner: start at the beginning, and end at the end.

Each spread can also be read as a standalone idea, or you can follow any one of the three footnotes to a page where a related subject is discussed.*

We won't tell; it's not cheating.

Choose your own adventure.

*For all other concepts (eg. *"book"*, *"read"*) please refer to your previous life experience, as mediated through your local cultural norms, some of which may be addressed herein.

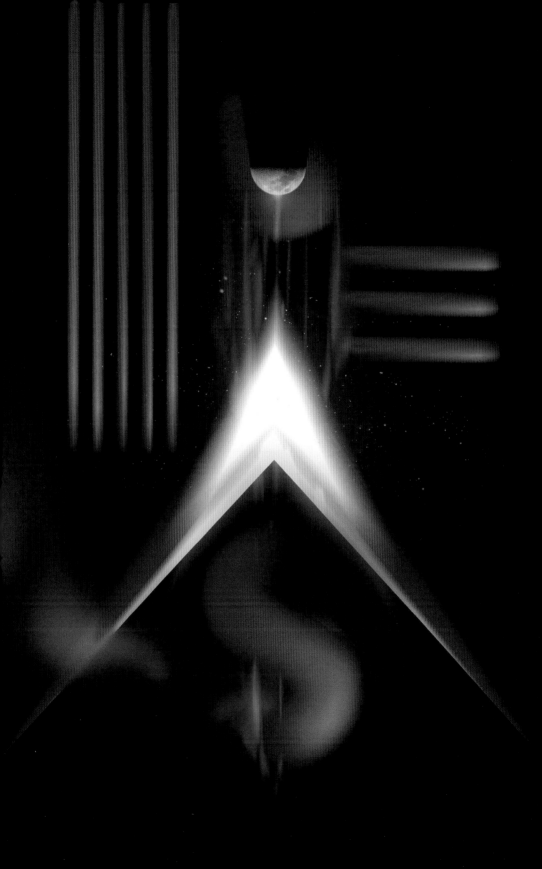

this is an idea

Or to be more precise, it's a *symbol* that *represents* an idea.

Almost *everything* can represent *something.* In fact, it's very hard to find anything, whether natural or man-made, that represents *nothing* – that has or has had no symbolic value whatsoever to someone, somewhere, at some point in time.

If you can find one of these rare things, it represents one thing and one thing only – *itself.*

is this an idea?

Would an image of a modern energy-saving bulb work in this context just as well?

Or do we need our lightbulb to look as generic, as "light-bulb-like" as possible?

Many common symbols in use today reference outdated or archaic forms:

TEACHER   **TELEPHONE**

When the form becomes too unfamiliar, the connection between symbol and meaning can break – and a new symbol is needed.

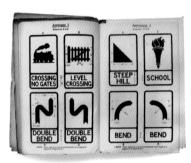

The exception occurs when the symbol is in such wide use and the connection is so strong that even what has become a seemingly arbitrary connection between symbol and meaning still holds.*

BARBER

Of course, it would be impractical to create a new symbol for every new thing we needed to symbolise. Wouldn't it be better to create a basic, simple set of symbols that could be combined in different ways to represent almost any idea or thing you wished?

A set of *meta-symbols?*

They'd need to be simple, easy to draw and easy to recognise . . .

* Medieval barbers also performed bloodletting. The red and white stripes represent bloodied and clean bandages.

how to symbolise any symbol

The series of simple, easy to draw shapes opposite, either alone or in combination, represent sounds uttered by the human voice.

Rearrange this set of symbols to represent any idea.

Proviso: Some ideas may be easier to represent than others. Unintended complications, simplifications and miscommunications may ensue.

Symbols may vary from country to country. Please adjust according to your local context.

The alphabet is a representation of a representation of a representation - a graphic notation describing an oral notation (speech) describing a mental representation or state.

The invention of printing with moveable type inaugurated the popularisation and democratisation of the written word, and the first great international spread of that which the word encodes – *ideas.*

"[Printing is the] industrialisation of language"
— Phil Baines

The written word turns a conversation into a monologue. It has authority and presence; it does not change its mind. Through it the dead speak to us, the distant is made close at hand.

The power of the Word.

"Give me 26 lead soldiers and I will conquer the world."
— Benjamin Franklin

abcdefghijklm
nopqrstuvwxyz
ABCDEFGHIJK
LMNOPQRSTU
VWXYZ
1234567890
!?@#$£%&*().,

word up

The written word, just as the spoken word before it that it codifies, has evolved to try and match the richness of our thoughts.

Ideas for which no word exists are either suppressed or only communicated with difficulty – which is why we constantly invent new words and distort and evolve the meanings of others as needed.

"Language is a virus."
— William Burroughs

Like a virus, strains of language evolve differently in different cultures or in geographically isolated areas, taking on a local colour and finally developing to the point where they are incomprehensible to outsiders.

Like new species, they have evolved to the point of mutual incompatibility.

Just as lengthy combinations of the four chemical letters of DNA, the genetic alphabet – *guanine, adenine, thymine* and *cytosine* – code for genes, so letters in combination code for words, which in turn build the syntactical equivalent of molecules – sentences. Letters have little meaning in and of themselves; it is how they are put together that is important.

Meaning, like life, only begins to emerge at the molecular level.

Gatc

gesture is language

Pictured opposite is a hand sign for 'bullshit': the index and little finger of one hand are raised to mimic bulls' horns, while the other hand alternately clenches and spreads wide its fingers.

Try it – it can be very expressive.

Before the written and spoken word there existed the *call* and the *gesture;* vocalisation and body language are found throughout the animal kingdom.

Signing is a human language that is visual rather than acoustic - and it is transmitted not only via the hands, but by the face and body too. Mimicry can sometimes more directly resemble, or map, the subject matter than spoken language; it is so useful that everyday conversation is still strongly reinforced by gesture. This extra postural layer can communicate meaning *even when a body is notably absent* – for example, when you've just been stood up.

The 'gestural theory' suggests that a form of signing preceded verbalised language. The shift to spoken communication may have arisen to free up the hands for other tasks. Spoken language can also function over a larger distance, or in terrain where individuals cannot see each other.

It can operate over even larger distances if you have a mobile.

Gesture is so embedded in the way we communicate that we find it hard *not* to use it – even in situations when, as on the telephone, it is completely invisible to the recipient.

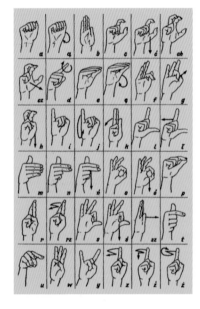

Above: Polish signing alphabet. Signing has local languages and dialects just as written language

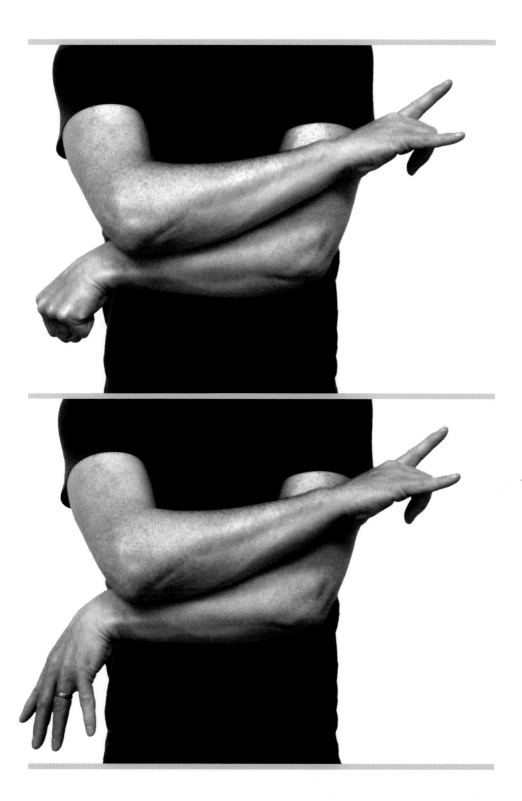

pre-guistic graff tags

Today humans, the only surviving members of the genus *Homo,* are the dominant species on our planet. We have somehow cleared a cognition gap between us and our next closest relatives; like a major planet, we have gravitationally emptied the space around us.

But it was not always so. *Neandertals* and *Homo Sapiens* coexisted, sometimes in close geographic proximity, for around 10,000 years. Related in terms of physiognomy, they shared the same habitats, and even interbred.

Did they also share a culture?

Complex culture and the ideas that travel through it are now a uniquely human phenomenon. Mediated by language, that language first took form in the spoken word.

The spoken word is the powerful tool that first enabled more complex social webs of interaction to form.

"The spoken word was the first technology by which man was able to let go of his environment in order to grasp it in a new way."
— Marshall McLuhan

Just as the call and the gesture predate formalised speech, so the precursor to the innovation of the written word is abstract or symbolic mark-making.

To produce the ancient silhouettes opposite, dye made from chewed vegetable matter was sprayed from the mouth over the splayed hand.

The artist's signature.

The history of art is the archaeology of culture.

Opposite: Cave paintings from Cueva de las Manos (Cave of the Hands), Santa Cruz, Argentina.

externalisation

The man-made, or man-altered, environment is now the familiar environment that surrounds us.

There are very few 'raw' environments left on earth. The land has been ordered, parcelled up, rationalised.

It was not always this way.

This artificial structure we find around us is our own. Like any record, it can be read and interpreted – a story written on the landscape.

Any physical record of a creative act, be it a work of art or a ploughed field, can be seen as a representation of an idea.

By externalising an idea, we get a better view of what it actually is.

To externalise something is to actualise it in the physical world. *Build it, make it, speak it, plough it.*

Then it is possible to *experience it - look at it, touch it, hear it, walk around it.* Once externalised, given a physical shape, it is now part of the input system, part of the previously raw environment.

We can even return to it later - its physicality preserves it in a kind of shared 'working memory', to be developed or reconsidered at leisure, over an extended timespan.

Thus externalised ideas develop, becoming raw material for new ideas, in a never-ending feedback loop – a process that occurs whenever one acts upon the world.

. . . subjective › objective › subjective › objective . . .

"L'existence précède l'essence." [Existence precedes essence] — Sartre

"Essence precedes existence" — Avicenna

We constantly create the language with which we speak to ourselves anew.

sign and signified

X=X. The representation of an idea by an imitation, a reproduction, an icon.

The realisation that *X need not = X* is a powerful conceptual breakthrough.

Arbitrary sounds and shapes can now be assigned meanings in new, non-representational, symbolic relationships. They can even be structured into a grammar to express ever more complex and abstract ideas.

Sophisticated language emerges.

This useful foray into non-representationalism has a downside, however: it necessitates that sender and receiver each understand the codes that are being used. For the first time, these codified, non-representational relationships are not immediately obvious and so need to be *learned.* For the most part, their very arbitrariness means they are not comprehensible to cultural outsiders – those who speak a different language, for example.

When anything can potentially be used to symbolise anything else, meaning is reliably transmitted only within a shared context.

Within a given culture, a symbol's ubiquity and familiarity means its arbitrary nature is not always apparent. Isolated tribes can be surprised to find out that people in the next valley speak an entirely different and incomprehensible language.

There are many other arbitrary aspects of culture that can seem completely natural and self-evident – *to those brought up within it.*

This disengagement of direct causal connection between sign and signified, the breaking of the representational link, can have unintended side effects. In a culture used to arbitrary relationships, causal rationality can have a slippery purchase.

Sometimes it pays to step outside your local set of assumptions and look at things from the outsider's viewpoint.

graphic esperanto

The written word has evolved by moving from more elaborate and realistic pictorial representations to codified, symbolic abstraction. This change is driven by functional necessity.

Unlike formal carved or illuminated inscriptions, any useful everyday writing system has got to be *fast* and *simple to use.*

The early alphabet only contained *capitals* – what we now know as *lower case* evolved later from a cursive, hand-drawn style developed for writing with a quill-pen on papyrus or parchment. Txt spk is an even more recently invented shorthand.

This 'format conversion bottleneck' – the necessary conversion of raw experience to fit the reduced formalised capabilities of a certain medium, for example writing – is essentially a *bandwidth* problem.

Online, this trend is now reversing. As bandwidth restrictions evaporate, we are returning to graphically rich environments, ones where symbols are again becoming more like their real-world counterparts.

Websites now routinely incorporate sound and animation. Immersive on-line environments like *World of*

Warcraft and *Second Life* provide virtual 3-D spaces in which social and business transactions can occur. Communications media are beginning to resemble the real world more and more closely.

As the actual interfaces between the real and the virtual become invisibly integrated into our everyday lives, perhaps these symbols will merge with the actualities that inspired them. In an 'augmented reality', real objects could function according to their virtual symbolic value and the world would be overlaid with causal agency once more.

We will have moved away from realistic depictions to abstract, codified representations and back again.

Press here to hear this read aloud:

Press here to see the movie version:

EGYPTIAN c.3000 BC

SEMITIC c.1500 BC

PHOENICIAN c.1000 BC

GREEK c.600 BC

ROMAN 113 CE

CALIFORNIAN 1984

CALIFORNIAN 1991

CALIFORNIAN 1997

CALIFORNIAN 1999

CALIFORNIAN 2002

the new hieroglyphics

Unlike the engineering constraints imposed on Isambard Kingdom Brunel by his construction materials – iron, steel and wood – or the self-imposed ideological constraints of the modernist architect, in the digital realm form is free of such practical constraint.

Form is no longer dictated by the materials used or the mechanics of manufacture.

In the digital realm, form no longer *follows* function; form *illustrates* function.

The function is *communication,* the form symbolic, the content meaning.

Wastebaskets, paint pots, pencils and other icons are busy chasing the dial telephone and teacher's mortar board from physical space into ideaspace.

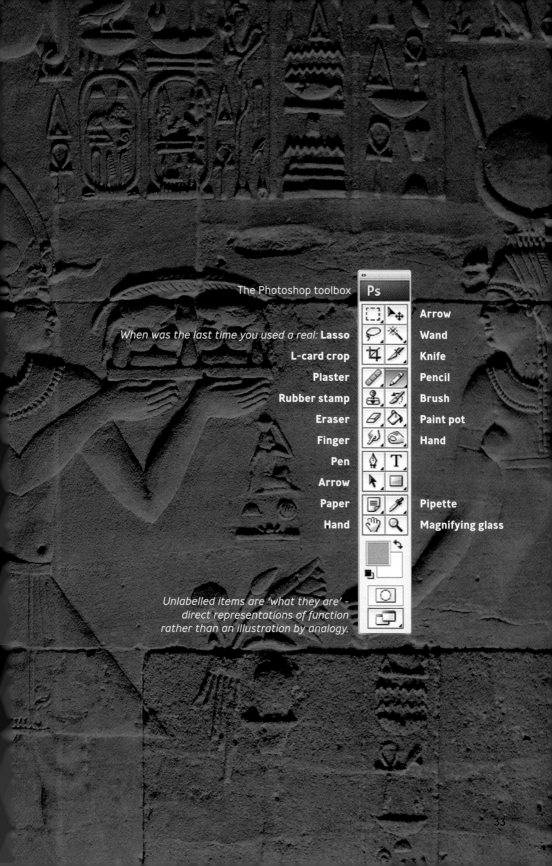

The Photoshop toolbox

When was the last time you used a real: **Lasso**

L-card crop

Plaster

Rubber stamp

Eraser

Finger

Pen

Arrow

Paper

Hand

Arrow

Wand

Knife

Pencil

Brush

Paint pot

Hand

Pipette

Magnifying glass

*Unlabelled items are 'what they are' –
direct representations of function
rather than an illustration by analogy.*

33

styling your symbolic symbols

ABCDEFGHIJ
KLMNOPQR
STUVWXYZ.
1234567890

The meaning of words can be further enhanced by the *style* of the letters.

This font you are reading is called **Ministry**. It has seven weights, from thin to **heavy**, plus *italics*. It is based on original designs for British road signs first introduced in 1933, and tends to communicate a clear, informational and formal British tone, even to readers who are unfamiliar with its history.

The 'Start Here' title on page 9 is set in **Dukane**, a type digitised from vintage microfiche film found at the New York Public Library. The source material's scratched eroded character – its 'degradation signature' – has been emphasised and preserved in perfectly reproduced imperfection.

The type style can thus enhance the clarity of the content – or comment on it, or even *contradict* it. The most versatile fonts are almost invisible; they're designed to be.

The style enhances the message.

A typeface is a representation of a representation of a representation of a representation.

Everyone who can write has designed one typeface: *their own handwriting*.

Based on the universal model, it still has room for personal expression, your own 'tone of voice'.

If letters are the particle physics of written language, then words are the chemistry, sentences the biology.

34

formality

Hate

Neutrality?

LOVE

WOW

strength

ELEGANCE

PIERCE

FILMOTYPE ZANZIBAR

HEATWAVE

PAYLOAD

FREEHAND 591

MOTTER FEMINA

BATTERY PARK

HELVETICA REGULAR

OUTLANDER

me old china

If language is a shared code that enables communication within a group, whether intentionally or not, it also *excludes* those outside the group.

If you don't speak French, then French is a secret code known only to those who have learned the local rules.

There are hidden codes in this book.

The 'Aricebo message' (left) was beamed into space in the direction of the M13 globular star cluster from the Aricebo radio telescope in 1974. Written by Frank Drake, with Carl Sagan and others, it is designed to be read by extraterrestrials – beings with whom we have no shared culture whatsoever.

While there could be no common *cultural* language, we should share a universal *natural* one - *mathematics.* When the semiprime string of 1,679 zeros and ones is arranged in a grid of 73 rows and 23 columns, an image appears. Can you read it?*

While some codes are *accidentally* comprehensible only within a certain tribe or subculture, some, like Palare or cockney rhyming slang, are specifically designed to exude non-members.

"There was me, that is Alex, and my three droogs, Pete, Georgie, and Dim, and we sat in the Korova Milkbar trying to make up our rassoodocks what to do with the evening."
— Anthony Burgess,
A Clockwork Orange

There are many ancient languages that remain undeciphered because we have no Rosetta Stone, no codecracking wheel, to provide a solution.

A case in point is the Phaistos Disc, a tablet of fired clay dating to the middle or late Minoan Bronze Age (2nd millennium BC). It is covered on both sides with a spiral of stamped symbols. Its meaning remains unknown, making it one of the most famous mysteries of archaeology.

From Caesar's code, through second world war Enigma codes to modern digital encryption methods and even street gang handsigns, some languages are specifically designed to only be read by those we choose to communicate with.

*Solution on page 226

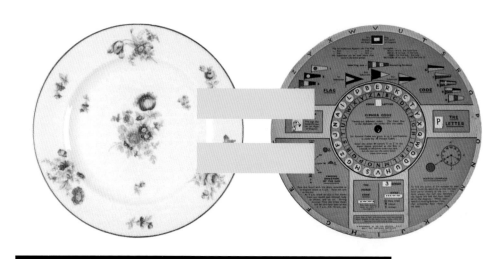

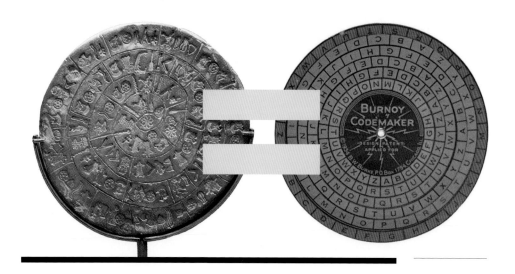

Bottom left: 'Face A' of the Phaistos Disc,
the Héraklion Archaeological Museum, Crete, Greece.

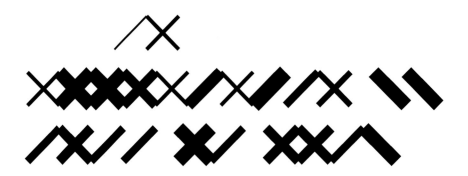

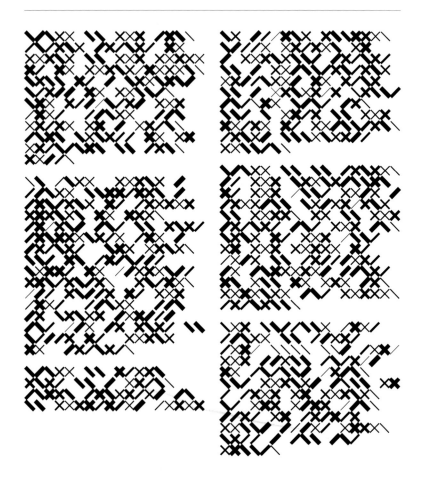

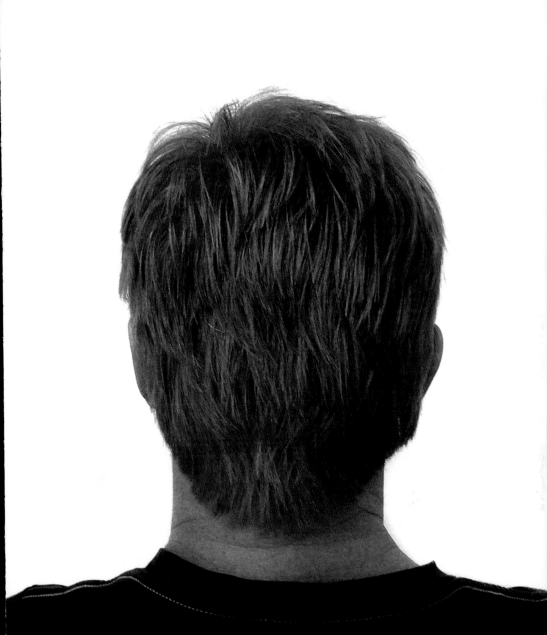

the tyranny of content

Repeat a random word aloud.

Very quickly, it will lose its meaning and become just a sound – as if it's an unknown word from an unknown language.

By stripping a word of its meaning, returning it to its abstract nature, its basic form is revealed; it stands bare, devoid of the function for which culture has appropriated it.

Without signification, it simply *sounds like a sound.*

Are we sometimes more intrigued by the form than the content?

Or does form have a content all its own?

The appreciation and production of sounds for their own aesthetic value has a name: *music.*

Music is primarily concerned with its internal self-reflective, non-representational structures – *the beat, the tune, the formal composition.*

Though sometimes deemed to be representational even without the overlay of lyrics or other signposted meaning, the abstract nature of music can still pack a serious emotive punch.

Strangely, while politicians might validate their policies by boasting of their support of the arts, the arts often believe they must be political in order to be of value.

Of all the arts, however, historically music is the one most comfortable with *abstraction,* comfortable with the inherent value of exploring its self-referential structure for its own sake.

It is what it is.

"Shoo-doo-shoo-bee-ooo-bee".
— Sarah Vaughan

"Louie-ooie-la-la-la".
— Betty Carter

"Choo-choo-wah, choo-choo-wah, shooby-doo-wah"
— Perry Como

where freedom is a slogan

PLEASE BIVE US
NWAT WE T

Outside the cultural context in which a message was created it can easily lose its meaning; its *is-ness* reasserts itself.

What it does retain is an evocative atmosphere of the 'other': an *alien glamour*.

The appropriated slogan as contentless fashion statement.

FREE

ME ANIR FREEDOMS:

FREEDOM BERELG

FEAN ARE FREE

A YOU V

42

FREEDOM T

HAK BEST!!

DOM

FREEDOM OF SPEECE

N, FREEDOM FROM

OM FROM NANT.

AR FOR

Above: Actual T-shirt photographed on a Hong Kong street

what shape is an idea?

Because novelty is sometimes hard to assimilate, we tend to view a new idea initially as a variation or development of an old familiar idea.

Clothing the new in the guise of the old gives us clues as to its function and meaning.

The true shape of an idea only becomes apparent later on, when it has found its own natural form. Until then, we operate by analogy. There will be a lot of the past in the future, acting as our guide.

Change the shape too fast, and the perceived symbolic connection to the intended function can become lost.

Early cars (from *carriage, cart*) resembled the horse-drawn variety. Only slowly did the shape of the car as we understand it today develop a language of its own, become its own symbol.

The *Waverley*'s roof was tall enough to accommodate a lady's hat. Nowadays, she'd be lying almost horizontal in a bright red Ferrari.

Some ideas, such as the electric car, are still waiting for their time to come – both the *Waverley* and the *Sinclair C5* had the plug unceremoniously pulled on them.

We employ the symbols of the past to signpost the future.

Because we can see where we've been but not where we're going, certain Pacific tribes have traditionally believed that we face the past – and have our backs to tomorrow.

"We look at the present through a rearview mirror; we walk backwards into the future."
— Marshall McLuhan

44

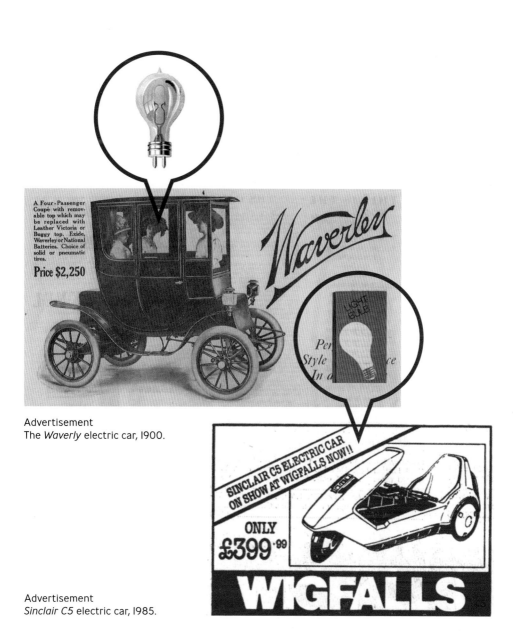

A Four-Passenger Coupé with removable top which may be replaced with Leather Victoria or Buggy top. Exide, Waverley or National Batteries. Choice of solid or pneumatic tires.

Price $2,250

Waverley

LIGHT BULB

Per
Style   ce
In a

Advertisement
The *Waverly* electric car, 1900.

SINCLAIR C5 ELECTRIC CAR ON SHOW AT WIGFALLS NOW!!

ONLY
£399·⁹⁹

WIGFALLS

Advertisement
Sinclair C5 electric car, 1985.

emergent ideas

How much processing power – in other words, how *bright* – do you need to be to have an idea?

The number of connections in the internet could be approaching the number of connections in the human brain (depending on how you measure it), which coincidentally is close to the total number of people now alive on the planet. If intelligence is simply an *emergent property of complexity,* as some have postulated, interesting things might be about to happen.

"Can you see what it is yet?"
— Rolf Harris

Just as in the example of the 'idea externalised', the ongoing *subjective › objective › subjective* feedback loop is theorised to have an entirely *internal* counterpart – each neuron, each department in the brain talking and listening to the others in turn. If consciousness is simply an emergent property, it is the sum result of these neuronal processes – and the ideas that we are aware that we 'have' are simply the *fittest*, those that rise to the surface of an ocean of competing notions.

As these ideas build over time, preserved in memory one upon the other, an internalised sense of *self* emerges and evolves.

Are you a *good idea?*

More accurately, the brain's function is not simply a product of its complexity but of its *connectivity.* Connectivity produces an internal responsive feedback loop, and as any musician will tell you, feedback is what you need in order to *"know what it is you're doing".*

The idea could be seen as the basic unit of consciousness. You are what you know.

This process whereby certain ideas come to dominate happens not only internally, in our individual consciousnesses, but also *externally,* in the interpersonal connectivity we share outside the confines of the brain – in *culture.*

Cohesive emergent behaviours can spontaneously appear in groups of independent but closely linked individuals without any central coordination. This emergent behaviour, dubbed 'flocking', or 'entrainment', is familiarly seen in birds but is also apparent in many types of human behaviour. A learner driver is told to "keep up with the traffic", as if the traffic was an entity in itself and not a collection of other drivers, all of whom may also be "keeping up with the traffic".

As the idea is shared, in a way *so is consciousness itself.* No one person is in charge because decision-making has become a 'distributed computing' process:

The idea is in charge.

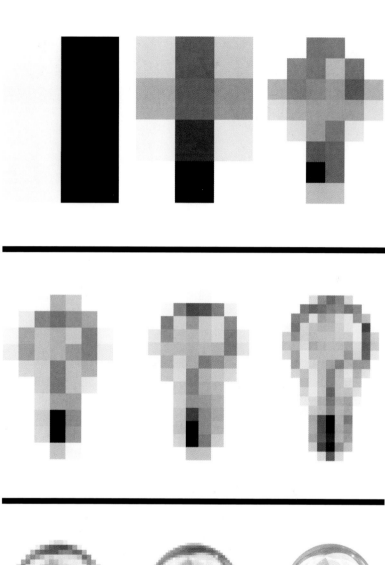

47

does a camera look like this?

What appears to be a coherent 'entity', at whatever scale, whether it be a culture, a flock, a mob, a human body, a human brain, a cell or an atom – is actually made of many smaller similar parts; each is closely interconnected to its fellows in an intimate feedback dance, simply on different scales.

The behaviour of the mob, whether in the January sales or at a lynching, illustrates powerfully how individual volition can be subsumed into the group, how the *idea* can take control.

'Flocking' also makes entrained groups susceptible to being nudged or lead in one direction or the other by outside forces, be they individuals – 'shepherds' who stand outside the group – or by highly infectious ideas.

Ideas shape culture.

In a secular democracy, the prevailing cultural mores - the shared values, ethical codes, social structures and attitudes – naturally evolve from the free exchange of ideas between the people who make up the culture; a loose consensus emerges, which changes, adapts, and is refined by feedback, discussion, protest, legislation, argument, gossip and generational change.

The jury of our peers.

A culture could be defined as the sum of the ideas a group, whether a nation, corporation or social circle, have. In fact, sharing a common set of ideas can now easily become the defining aspect of group membership, trumping geographical location or nationality.

"The Web has led to all kinds of new social groups . . . simply because we have been extraordinarily constrained by geography and history."
— Peter Andreas Thiel, PayPal founder

In the new cultural environment that is being shaped by an emerging global connectivity, your existing operational worldview may well be obsolete. Are you still running out-of-date wetware that could leave you open to infection by new and dangerous ideas?

Are you walking backwards into the future?

Time to upgrade.

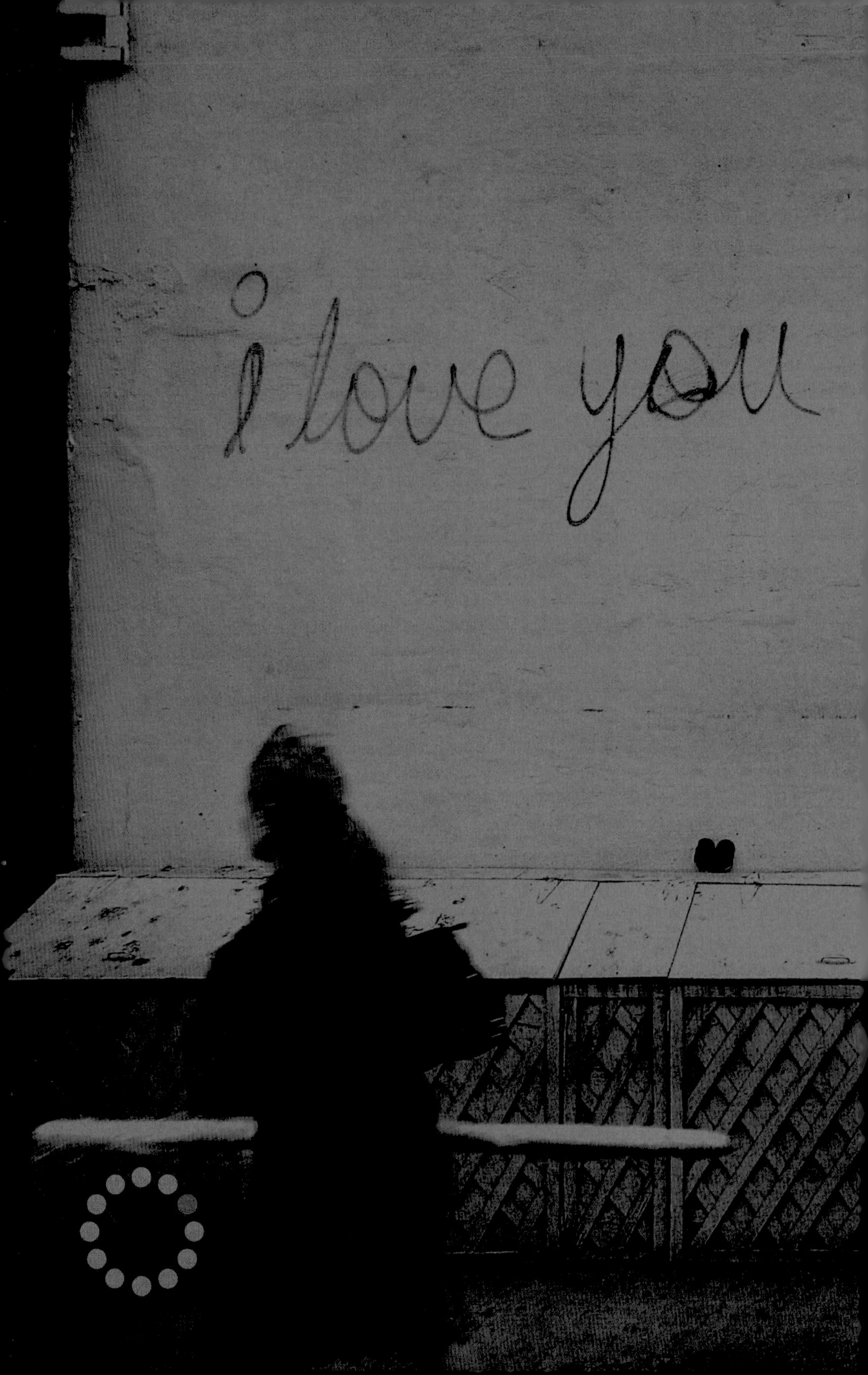
i love you

the oral tradition

Humans, not being telepathic and therefore not possessed with the power to transfer ideas directly from brain to brain, need to use more indirect methods of communication.

For an idea to be carried from one mind to another it requires a medium to travel through - a *delivery mechanism*. Verbal, gestural, written. Filmed, recorded, reproduced.

This book is a delivery mechanism.

Before the written word there was the spoken word – *the voice*. Our stories, our history, were passed down from generation to generation as the *oral tradition*.

Part fact, part interpretation, these narratives helped us structure and interpret reality. Sometimes they were even mistaken *for* reality.

Let me tell you a story . . .

do you get me?

"The words of language, as they are written or spoken, do not seem to play any role in my mechanism of thought"
— Albert Einstein

Only when it comes to the *expression* of thought do words come into play.

The spoken word has evolved to try and accurately convey the complexity and richness of our thoughts.

To be effectively communicated, a thought, *an idea,* needs to be reformatted several times on its journey from mind to mind.

"Conventional words or other signs have to be sought for laboriously in a second stage."
— Albert Einstein

Like all methods of reproduction, it can be subject to distortion, noise and misinterpretation.

The words themselves may be lacking: ideas for which no word exists are either unconsciously suppressed or only communicated with some difficulty.

The conversion from thought to language may be distorted or inaccurate; the reconversion from language to understanding in the mind of the recipient likewise.

I know you think you understood what I said, but what you heard was not what I meant.

Newly coined phrases or words – *neologisms* – will enter the popular lexicon readily if they have an immediate application, if they represent an idea looking for expression, or if, like lower case script, they just make communication faster and simpler.

Thus does language evolve, IMHO.

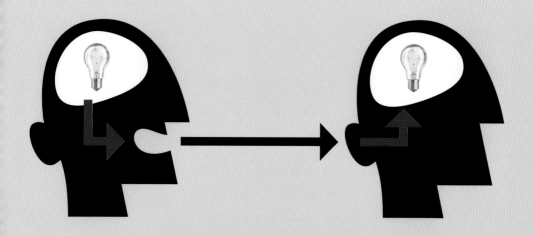

= FORMAT CONVERSION

signal to noise

Spectator I:
"I think it was 'Blessed are the cheesemakers'".
Mrs. Gregory:
"Aha, what's so special about the cheesemakers?"
Gregory:
"Well, obviously it's not meant to be taken literally; it refers to any manufacturer of dairy products."
— Monty Python's *The Life of Brian*

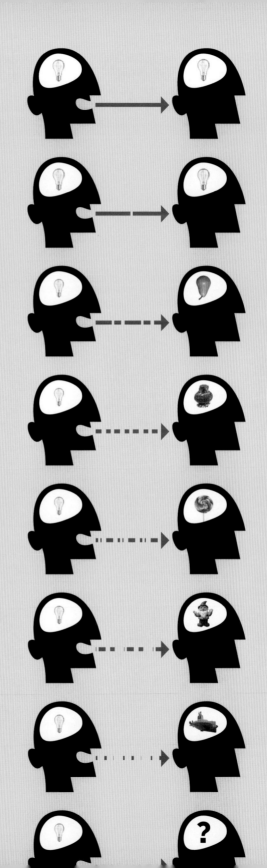

telepathy

Would direct, mediumless mind-to-mind communication necessarily convey ideas precisely, without distortion? What might it be like to have someone else's ideas?

When every person is effectively an island, much of our inner thought processes are never communicated.

Can you keep my secrets?

Telepathy could cause our sense of self to unravel as we began to seep into each other's minds. We might find it hard to tell where I end and you begin.

Our sense of existence as a discrete unit of being has much to do with the impermeability of the vessel we inhabit: *our body.* Our self can only draw in the 'other' via the senses, only escape the confines of our physical body through a feat of translation and reinterpretation.

However, this prison can be breached. The body is already being augmented by technology, and this trend will continue.

"By the 2030s, the nonbiological portion of our intelligence will predominate."
— Ray Kurzweil

If the brain can be mapped and the mind encoded and downloaded, Kurzweil believes humanity could transcend its limited biology.

This digital immortality might not be exactly what we imagine, however. As digital entities we will be subject to all the manipulations now familiar to us from the world of digitised music and art: we will be edited, enhanced, duplicated, corrupted and compressed with lossy algorithms. We will be illegally downloaded, remixed, 'mashed up' with other entities, reimagined, sold, given away, stolen, back engineered and decompiled.

We will be hacked and hijacked.

In gaining this form of immortality, our identities could be fundamentally transformed. Will we inevitably lose our sense of *self* and become unindividuated parts of a much larger whole, an *overmind?*

"I will not be pushed, filed, stamped, indexed, briefed, debriefed or numbered! My life is my own!"
— No.6, *The Prisoner*

Behind the firewall of our senses, we may feel we are protected from such manipulations – *but ideas which can jump the format conversion barrier have been hijacking our minds ever since language was invented.*

Remember to lock the back door to your brain.

error corection

Data transmission is subject to corruption through noisy media, and nature and humankind have both designed *error correction* mechanisms to circumvent this inevitable signal degradation.

Most digital codes incorporate error correction techniques. Barcodes use a 'check digit'; it is usually the last number in the code string, and is computed using an algorithm from the other digits in the data. CD players, high speed modems, deep space probes and cellular phones all use similar techniques to combat unwanted loss and distortion.

Similarly, DNA incorporates biological error-correction mechanisms to overcome random mutations and transcription mistakes before they can seriously affect a gene's functionality.

The error-correcting algorithm will attempt to reconstruct the lost portions of the message from the remaining information – *within certain limitations*. Every error correction method has a point beyond which there is simply not enough information for an accurate reconstruction.

In social situations – a crowded room, for example, where background noise can be overwhelming – error correction can be derived from other cues: lip reading or body language, for example.

This additional layer of information can even help us construct a more nuanced interpretation of events, even when the 'noise' is minimal.

In these cases, more information is extracted from a signal than the sender may intend - *signal enhancement*.

7 59606 06689 6

data
restoration

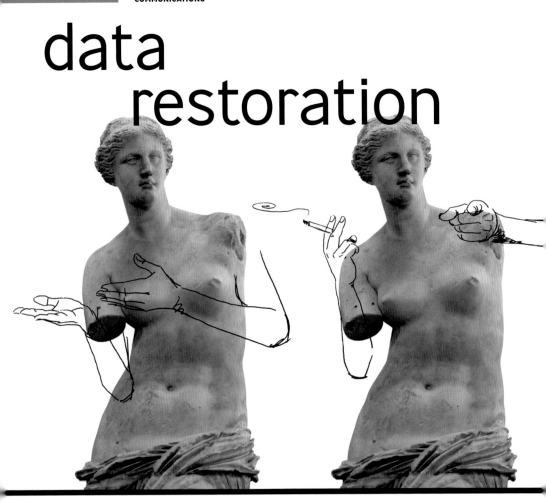

Theoretical extrapolations A-D.

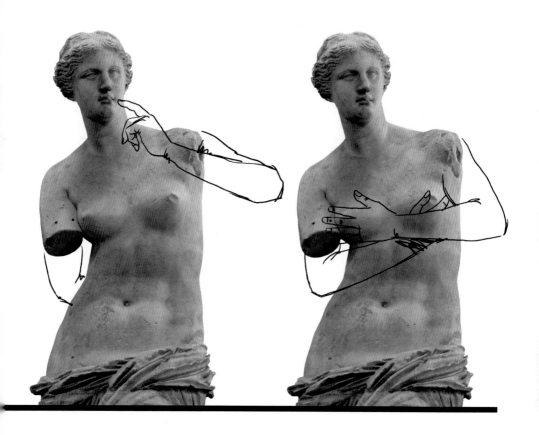

time as noise

As time passes, the context changes, and our ability to correctly decipher the original meaning of a message can be severely hindered. Our frame of reference is simply too dissimilar from the original frame to be useful.

"A painting is never finished."
— Pablo Picasso

Thus even perfectly preserved messages can still change in their perceived meaning.

That particularly human obsession, *etiquette* – the codified rules of social engagement, the pressure to build social capital with peers in a highly structured fashion – survives best in cultures where interpersonal relationships are formal and at one remove, or arranged through intermediaries.

It's who you know, you know.

Outside the frame of a specific cultural context, some social norms can seem counterintuitive and even absurd.

And over time, the rules of the game can change. We are all time travellers, travelling forward into the future at a steady speed of precisely 60 minutes an hour, 24 hours a day, 365¼ days a year.

Callers should always be provided with cards. A gentleman should carry them loose in a convenient pocket; but a lady may use a card case. No matter how many members of the family you call upon, you send in but one card. Where servants are not kept, and you are met at the door by the lady herself, of course there is no use for a card. If you call upon a friend who has a visitor, send in but one card; but if they are not at home, leave a card for each.

Calls of pure ceremony are sometimes made by simply handing in a card. When a stranger arrives in the city, he should send his card, with directions, to those whom he expects to call upon him. Otherwise his presence might remain for some time unknown. If a stranger of your own profession comes to the city, you should call upon him even though you do not know him.

A card may be made to serve the purpose of a call. It may be sent in an envelope, or left in person. In the latter case, one corner should be turned down if for the lady of the house. Fold the card in the middle if you wish to indicate that the call is on several, or all of the members of the family. Leave a card for each guest, should any be visiting at the house.

A card enclosed in an envelope, for the purpose of returning a call made in person, expresses a desire that visiting between the parties be ended. When such is not the intention, cards should not be enclosed in an envelope.

The cards of unmarried and married men should be small (about 1.25" by 3"). For married persons a medium size is in better taste than a large card. The engraving in simple writing is preferred, and without flourishes. Printed letters, large or small, are very commonplace, no matter what the type may be. The "Mr." before the name should be dispensed with by young men.

from
RULES OF ETIQUETTE & HOME CULTURE, 1882

gatekeeping the bottleneck

Access to the *media*, the means of communication outside one's immediate circle, has traditionally been concentrated in the hands of a small elite – an elite who act as *gatekeepers*.

The broadcasting companies are the gatekeepers of television content, the publishers gatekeepers of the printed word. The clergy are gatekeepers for God, the bouncer gatekeeper for the nightclub. The ruling party are gatekeepers for policy, the social elite gatekeepers of high society.

If you desired access to something, you needed to deal with the gatekeeper. Once in place, gatekeepers are hard to ignore - they are in a position of power, whether they chose it or not. More pertinently, their position is automatically bolstered and sustained by people's need to access the goal beyond. Unaccountability, then inefficiency, favouritism, bribery and corruption, tend to follow.

Any stratified society will develop restricted channels of access, and restricting channels of access will inevitably produce a stratified society.

This is all changing. Affordable and ubiquitous access to the Internet puts the power to publish - opinion, news, music, ideas, art, anything that can be reduced to ones and zeroes - *in everyone's hands*. Young or old, prince or pauper, Brahmin or Untouchable, all are on a level playing field. All it requires is time and effort.

The information superhighway is a hierarchy bypass.

Want to find a marriage partner, or a casual date? There are sites for that. Want to publish your blog? Sign up here. Want to start a business? Dotcoms are (mostly) booming. Want access to information, to a plurality of views? There's so much out there you'll need another type of gatekeeper, this time one *you* appoint, the *editor* - to filter it all for you.

This new accessibility has produced a phenomenal outpouring of creativity. Individuals or loose-knit groups can invest tens of thousands of man-hours for nothing more than the satisfaction of creation, or the building of 'social currency'. This phenomenon of horizontally shared user-generated content is dubbed Web 2.0.

Of course, the gatekeepers, those further up the hierarchy who are used to their privileged positions as arbiters of culture, might not see these new freedoms as necessarily a good thing.

The need to be nice is inversely proportional to the power you wield.

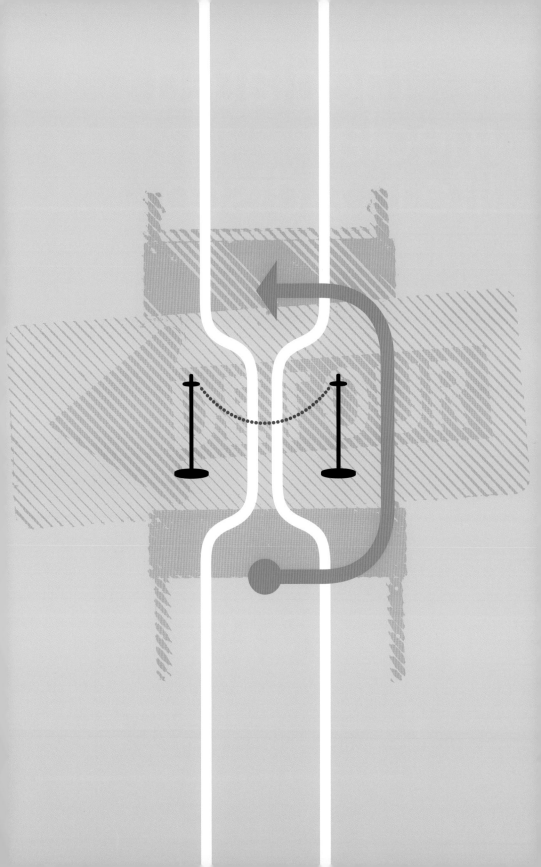

mediated media: life in a disco

Before disco, self-respecting musical venues boasted either a live band or a jukebox.

The DJ had not been invented.

Paris, 1953: at the *Whisky à Gogo,* a 24 year old Régine Zylberberg sets up two turntables so she can play music without interruption. This innovation signals the birth of the modern *discothèque*. (She also taught the Duke of Windsor the twist).

The idea that the public would listen, not to a live band, or even jukebox music of their own choosing, but to *pre-recorded music chosen by someone else* was a novel one.

Today almost everything we encounter has been recorded and played back. Very little of what we experience is actually *live*. Yet *live* is how life happens, and *live* was the only way, before technology permitted reproduction, life happened.

If most of what we see via the media is not live, it must be *edited:* sifted for value, interpreted and re-presented for our convenience. *We live in a disco, and the DJ is in charge.*

We choose our choosers like we choose our newspaper - they reflect our tastes, interests and prejudices.

The 'media jockey', or MJ, will be an autonomous software agent that seeks out material based on past choices. In delegating our choice-making to a trusted other, we also allow it a degree of control over us. Our horizons shrink in one direction as they expand in another.

With the surfeit of choice technology provides, exposure to novelty paradoxically becomes easier to avoid.

Who's on your playlist?

a surfeit of content

"One of the effects of living with electronic information is that we live habitually in a state of information overload. There's always more than you can cope with."
— Marshall McLuhan

We are all becoming information managers, deciding what we can and cannot afford to ignore.

To deal with this cacophony, an audience suffering from information surfeit tends to fracture into smaller and smaller specialist interest groups, where everyone shares a very similar set of values. This, of course, doesn't guarantee harmony – the smallest difference of opinion can create a new splinter group. Ultimately, we may all end up in a splinter group which consists of only one member – *ourselves.*

Our culture is no longer defined by our geographic location, our 'village', but by membership of a self-selecting 'global village' of like-minded people. The members of these 'supranational communities' are separated by distance, not difference.

Culture is no longer simply a function of locality.

Unique cultures develop in isolated communities, and ideas that seem 'normal' to those within the group may not fit the norms of wider society. The sheer excess of information in the 'global village' may thus not provide the usual normalising memetic checks and balances; indeed it may do quite the opposite.

In a billion internet users you will always find someone who agrees with you. Every interest, however obscure or extreme, is catered for.

In the modern electronic world it is still possible to be part of an isolated community, this time bound by the power of a shared worldview instead of the confines of a remote valley.

In a world swamped with an excess of information, what commodity is *rare?* Other than an intrinsic functional or artistic value, something has to be rare to have a monetary value. In a world of surfeit, the rarest commodity is your time.

Start charging for your attention.

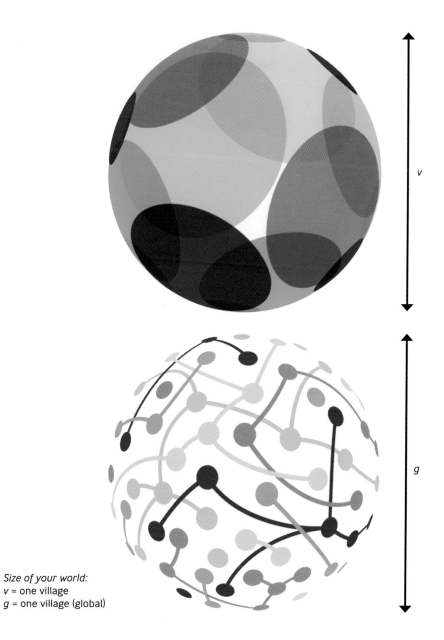

Size of your world:
v = one village
g = one village (global)

get the message?

While simplification is often necessary for the sake of clarity and comprehension, unearthing the essence of a message from a mound of complex information can often lead to oversimplification.

As anyone who has read an article on a subject they know intimately will attest, the need to impose a cohesive structure to an article – a beginning, middle and end – means certain awkward details tend to be left out.

This process is the written equivalent of the drift apparent in the *oral tradition*. Stories are polished in the retelling, like pebbles in a stream; details erode until the essential features are all that remain.

These essential features are those that tend to support the moral point or 'message' of the tale. If the tale is based on real events, the details of that source event that survive or take prominence are those that the storyteller or reporter finds useful; the elements which, though they may add verisimilitude, are irrelevant to the propagation of the 'message' will atrophy and fall away over time.

Anyone who has kept a diary will be familiar with this process. When first set down, a diarist struggles to remember and accurately recount the day's events, and is always aware they are streamlining and omitting, both intentionally via the above process and unintentionally through lapses in memory. The diarist is aware that the record is at best an approximation.

Upon rereading weeks or years later, however, the entry will be full of details that have since been forgotten – and so, because this is now the best record that remains, it trumps the fading memory which has meantime leapfrogged the diarist's written word into subjectivity.

In reducing complex issues to a simple, direct and memorable slogan, a similar process takes place. Any message, reduced to a flag, a chant or a call-to-arms, can be communicated very powerfully. But that persuasive power is achieved by the removal of detail and subtlety.

The edited highlights are all we recall.

72

SIMPLIFY
SIMPLIFY
SIMPLIFY

even better than the real thing

We are all in the movie of our lives.

A world where real experience can seem pale by comparison with media-delivered experience.

How many life-shaping insights have been delivered to you via books, films or television rather than by reality?

"Just living lines from books we've read, with atmospheres of days gone by . . ."
— Ultravox

Many spectators who are attending a live event will still watch the coverage on a portable TV for the close-ups, the edited highlights, the commentary, the on-screen statistics. Compared to the slow, unpredictable and unedited unfolding of real life, edited experience is concentrated, richer, sometimes more *real than real.*

Cut to the chase.

Do we now *prefer* experience to be mediated, to be reinterpreted for us? Or is it just that our new electronically extended horizon means seeing events with our own eyes is now rarer than seeing them via the camera's eye?

That we are completely familiar with this non-participatory involvement is illustrated by the humanly impossible acts of filmmaking's free-floating camera. We sit on the bonnet of a car looking at our main players, we zoom under bridges, through keyholes and hover, disembodied, over cities.

So accepted is this voyeuristic convention that it can seem strange when the actors acknowledge the camera, break the 'fourth wall' and look directly into the lens and hence our eyes. This acknowledgement of the audience – of *you* – steps outside the conventions we have set for ourselves, the *rules of the game.*

Conversely, the act of taking photographs, filming, or otherwise recording an event separates us from the event itself. Inserting a camera between ourselves and the world paradoxically distances us from the moment while preserving it. Aware that we are now watching ourselves watching, we record but can't participate.

This separation can also distance us from the emotive content, as reality collapses to the equivalent of a special effect. At one remove, it is possible to avoid the uncomfortable immediacy, the participatory overload, that life experienced first hand – that *really being there* – can entail.

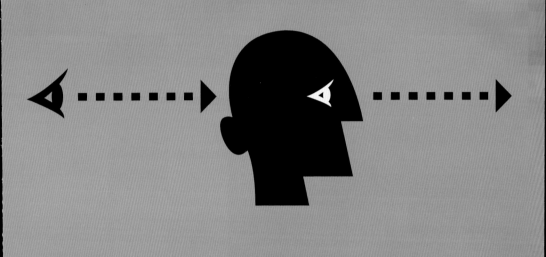
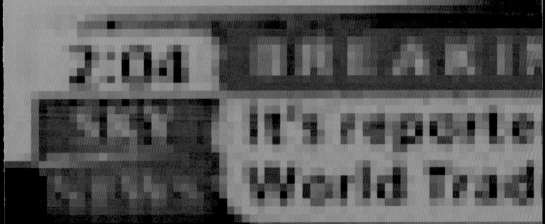

culture as memory

Culture acts as an externalised memory, an off-brain backup.

Language, art, song, writing and other means of externalising and preserving ideas permit cultural continuity; we can refer back to the experiences and memories of our forebears. Culture can develop over more than one lifetime, and innovations are not lost with their creators.

We can download our experience for the next generation.

Cultures eventually develop institutions to codify, promote and retain their ideas. With their formalised structures, they are designed to outlive individuals, and are capable of transmitting ideas uninterrupted over thousands of years as new generations are inducted to carry them forward, transient cells in the body politic.

Though these institutions can be surprisingly robust, inevitably they can also mutate or fail entirely. Many monuments from antiquity are the ruins of forgotten institutions, their memetic continuity broken. Just the physical shell remains, its original purpose obscure, its reconstruction educated guesswork.

New ideas supplant old; the monument becomes a palimpsest.

Memory is the thread of the story of our lives. From it we retroactively construct a tale of which we are the hero, the main player – even if we only have a walk-on part.

Our memories of past events are *reinterpreted* as time passes – they are distilled from specific recollections down to their essential symbolic essence.

A similar process happens in the wider culture: a move from *specifics* to *meaning,* from the *representational* to the *symbolic:* a process of *mythmaking.*

Events become more meaningful with the benefit of hindsight. The story unfolds as we look back on it.

Nostalgia works because we have the benefit of a retrospective overview; we feel comfortable because we understand the narrative and know how the story turns out. Embedded in life lived live, we are buffeted by vibrant detail; we are simply standing too close to events to discern their true shape.

notation precedes recording

Before *mechanical recording and reproduction,* there was *re-enactment.*

Theatre, dance, music – the live performance. *Painting, writing, sculpture* – the man-made representation.

Re-enactment is essentially recreation via the agency of mind rather than machine. The original needs to be studied, internalised, and then externalised once more. It is recreated with a greater or lesser fidelity according to skill or intention - it is *reinterpreted.*

Mechanical reproduction, by contrast, requires no human processing. It is achieved via technology: the machine listens without hearing, looks without seeing, records without interpreting, and privileges nothing.

In a pre-technological world, where there is no direct method of reproduction available – no film, sound recording or photography – information must be encoded via a *notation* that is later decoded by the performer tasked with the recreation.

As with the alphabet, a representation of speech, musical notation, for example, is a representation of sound.

Mechanised re-enactment is the transitional form: inspired by the punched cards of the Jacquard loom, early player-pianos represent not a true means of recording, but a *recorded means of re-enactment.*

The necessity of fitting a performance through the informational limitations of a notation – another *format conversion bottleneck* – means that, just like language, it has to take into account and even be shaped by the capabilities and limitations of the encoding medium.

Before mechanical reproduction, a piece was therefore defined by the *notation* rather than the *execution;* it was a formal composition with no definitive expression. Any expression was governed by the ability and range of the player and the instrument.

Mechanical recording allows the listener or viewer direct access to the intent of the creator. More than that, by bypassing the notation bottleneck, digital technology has become an instrument in its own right - the original performance can be cleaned up, finessed or even assembled entirely artificially, piece by piece, from scratch. The act of recording can become the 'performance'.

Opposite: player-piano punched card

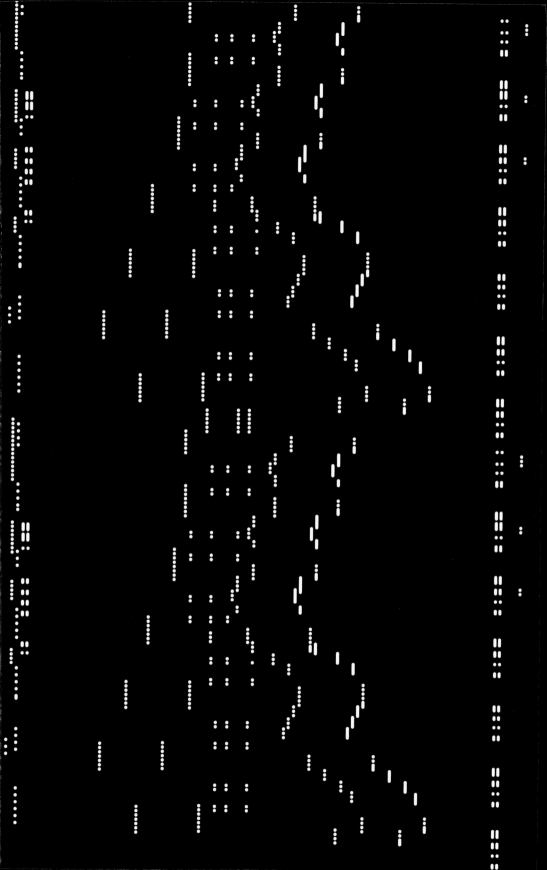

we are at the very beginning of recorded history

Chances are you have a few photographs of your grandparents and maybe one or two staged studio portraits of your great grandparents, but beyond that, birth, marriage and death certificates – the bare bones of existence – are the only surviving signposts on the route back into the past.

The exceptions to this general state of affairs were the aristocrats, the kings and queens, the privileged and the famous: history's movers and shakers.

Film, sound reproduction and stills photography, the familiar recording mechanisms that technology has provided us with, were all invented in the last 100 years, and only more recently have they become cheap and available to all – and thus not only ubiquitous but *democratic*.

The intimate details of the lives of 'average' people are now being routinely recorded and preserved in often mind-numbing detail. History is no longer the story of those who were rich or important enough to carve their conquests in stone or have their portrait painted in oils.

From the perspective of the grand sweep of history, *this has just happened.* Personal Records, Year One.

From here on, every mundane detail of every person's life can be preserved. A digital avalanche of photographs, email exchanges, blog entries and home videos are being produced, alongside the growing capacity of the state to document our lives through CCTV, our financial and legal transactions, and a wealth of other computerised and cross-referenced records.

There is now the flesh of character on the bare bones of Everyman. We are at the very beginning of democratically recorded history.

Your great-great-great grandchildren will know exactly what you did this summer.

Above: 'The Blue Marble', taken on December 7,
1972 by the crew of Apollo 17 en route to the Moon,
at a distance of 29,000 kilometers.

DUPLICATION, DUPLICATION, DUPLICATION

"Only an idea could spread so far"
— Mies van de Rohe

Affordable duplication, and the resultant spread of information, are the hallmarks of an industrialised culture.

The one-off nature of a hand-made object, while a necessity for monetary value in, for example, fine art, can be a liability when it comes to the spread of its *cultural* value.

An idea multiplied through conversation can travel further than you can shout.

An idea multiplied through the written word can travel further than a conversation.

An idea multiplied through the printed book can travel further than the written word.

An idea set free of physical form, digitised as pure information, where every copy is perfectly indistinguishable from the 'original', can travel further than a multitude of books.

As human beings, however, we are all limited editions of one.

But maybe in the future this too will change.

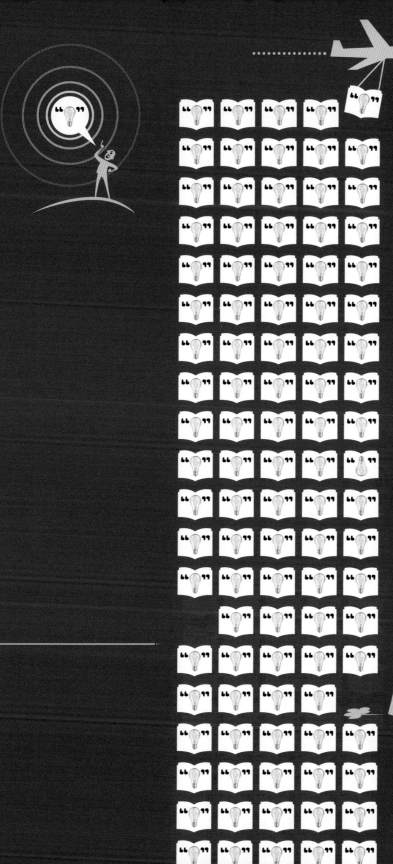

download me

Recorded content in a digital format can now exist free of a specific physical medium, the *vessel*.

Information in old vessels – *books, cassettes, records, videos* – could be easily duplicated, but duplication implied duplication of the physical vessel, the carrying medium, as well as the content.

This is no longer the case.

Set free from the medium, the message is the message.

RIP

RIP

RIP

RIP

RIP

RIP

RIP

RIP

RIP

RIP

convergence

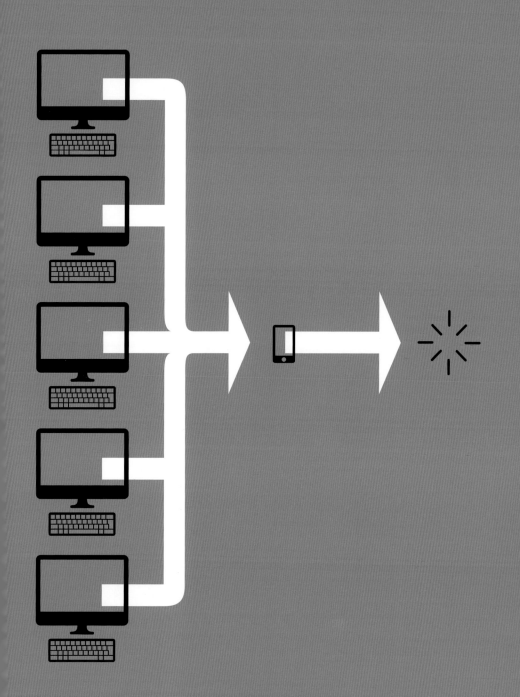

degradation signature

CDs skip, tapes stretch and hiss, vinyl crackles, jpegs look watery, film scratches.

Every medium has a unique way of malfunctioning - this is its 'degradation signature'.

Even the non-mechanical method of oral duplication suffers from signal degradation - just like the shifting vagaries of memory, it moves towards *meaning* and away from actuality, because *meaning* is the essence that gives a story its power and makes it more memorable.

Above: Malfunctioning BBC Ceefax page

By imperfect duplication and loss of detail we drift towards symbolism.

An expert can spot this tendency in the evolution of a narrative, just as a photographic expert can see the loss of clarity and detail in a reproduced print.

Now, in the digital realm, every copy is perfect. Unless we apply 'lossy' data compression techniques, each duplicate is an exact reproduction. There is no physical degradation – and, for digitally created work, *no unique original.*

high–fidelity reproduction

SEE IF YOU CAN COPY THIS PICTURE

▶ 90 DEGRADATION SIGNATURE
▶ 42 WHERE FREEDOM IS A SLOGAN
▶ 80 NOTATION PRECEDES RECORDING

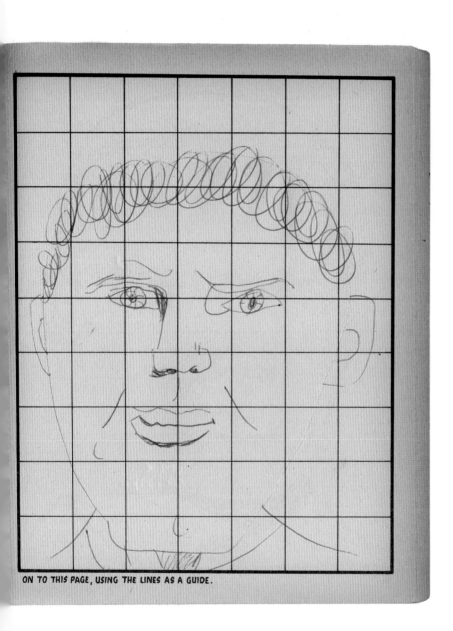

ON TO THIS PAGE, USING THE LINES AS A GUIDE.

extend yourself

Though we are mobile, we view the world from a fixed viewpoint.

However far you run, you can't get away from where you are.

We feel as if we are armchair travellers, sitting in the control rooms of our brains, looking out through the windows of our eyes. It is not possible to look through another's eyes, listen with another's ears, know *directly* another's thoughts.

However, though we may be confined within the frame of one body, that body is *extensible*. When driving, the mind's internal 'map' will extend to encompass the car, its physically extended body. We say *"I was hit!"* not *"My car was hit!"*

". . . Tools . . . ultimately turned the tables on their users. The origin of 'humanness' can be defined as that point in our evolution where these tools became the principle source of selection on our bodies and brains. It is the diagnostic of Homo Symbolicus."
— Terrence Deacon

In fact, *any tool we use is incorporated into our mind's map of ourselves.* Each tool is a technology that extends our body, and thus our sphere of direct influence.

"The wheel is an extension of the foot, the book an extension of the eye . . ."
— Marshall McLuhan

The impression, via technology, of being present at a distant location is called 'telepresence'. Could extending our senses fundamentally change our sense of self?

Imagine if, plugged into the Net, we could routinely look through the compound eye of a multitude of cameras, or channel sounds from any distant microphone, or gaze out at the surface of Mars via infra-red eyes mounted on rovers, or, via deep space probes, float over the gas giants of the outer solar system, listening to the falling dog-whistle of high-energy gamma rays.

And if this experience became the norm, where might we end up parking our real bodies once they had no reason to physically go anywhere?

"We become what we behold. We make our tools and then our tools make us."
— Marshall McLuhan

the meme

A *meme* is a *transmittable unit of information;* passed from person to person through imitation, education or indoctrination, it is a *"self-replicating unit of transmission"*.

"What's a meme made of? They're made of information, and can be carried in any physical medium. What's a word made of?"
— Dan Dennett

Coined by Richard Dawkins to help explain the evolution of ideas within a culture by analogy to the spread of *genes* within a population, memes, just like genes, evolve by natural selection, mutation, inheritance and competition. Some become extinct; others can become widespread.

Trends, fads, melodies, technologies and religions - all can be considered as memes.

Genes, being entirely physical, can only transfer information *vertically,* from generation to generation. Their transmission is limited by the location of the physical vehicle they inhabit - *the body.*

Memes can transfer information *horizontally,* and across large distances via carriers such as the Internet. Unlike genes, memes are transmittable via any medium capable of recording and relaying symbolic information: language, gesture, art, the written word, film, music, fashion.

Culture is primarily memetic, not genetic.

The internet provides a new and uniquely powerful delivery mechanism, one in which information – and its associated fads, scams and other viral phenomena – can reach millions in a very short time.

Memes are contagious.

Advances in modern medicine have effectively removed humankind from the pressures of natural selection, and in fact Susan Blackmore, author of *The Meme Machine,* posits that meme replication has almost completely overwhelmed the glacially slow rate of gene replication.

Crucially, unlike their biological counterparts, memes can even proliferate when they are detrimental to the very survival of their hosts.

1988, and one of the first internet virus hoaxes. Though the virus itself did not exist, the manner in which the message spread is itself viral. Email hoaxes such as these can mutate, as elements are added, deleted or otherwise customised; indeed, diagrams resembling evolutionary trees can be retroactively constructed that chart these modifications and their subsequent evolutionary fitness.

SUBJ: Really Nasty Virus
AREA: GENERAL (1)

I've just discovered probably the world's worst computer virus yet. I had just finished a late night session of BBS'ing and file treading when I exited Telix 3 and attempted to run pkxarc to unarc the software I had downloaded. Next thing I knew my hard disk was seeking all over and it was apparently writing random sectors. Thank god for strong coffee and a recent backup. Everything was back to normal, so I called the BBS again and downloaded a file. When I went to use ddir to list the directory, my hard disk was getting trashed again. I tried Procomm Plus TD and also PC Talk 3. Same results every time. Something was up so I hooked up to my test equipment and different modems (I do research and development for a local computer telecommunications company and have an in-house lab at my disposal). After another hour of corrupted hard drives I found what I think is the world's worst computer virus yet. The virus distributes itself on the modem sub-carrier present in all 2400 baud and up modems. The sub-carrier is used for ROM and register debugging purposes only, and otherwise serves no othr (sp) purpose. The virus sets a bit pattern in one of the internal modem registers, but it seemed to screw up the other registers on my USR. A modem that has been "infected" with this virus will then transmit the virus to other modems that use a subcarrier (I suppose those who use 300 and 1200 baud modems should be immune). The virus then attaches itself to all binary incoming data and infects the host computer's hard disk. The only way to get rid of this virus is to completely reset all the modem registers by hand, but I haven't found a way to vaccinate a modem against the virus, but there is the possibility of building a subcarrier filter. I am calling on a 1200 baud modem to enter this message, and have advised the sysops of the two other boards (names withheld). I don't know how this virus originated, but I'm sure it is the work of someone in the computer telecommunications field such as myself. Probably the best thing to do now is to stick to 1200 baud until we figure this thing out.

Mike RoChenle

memeword

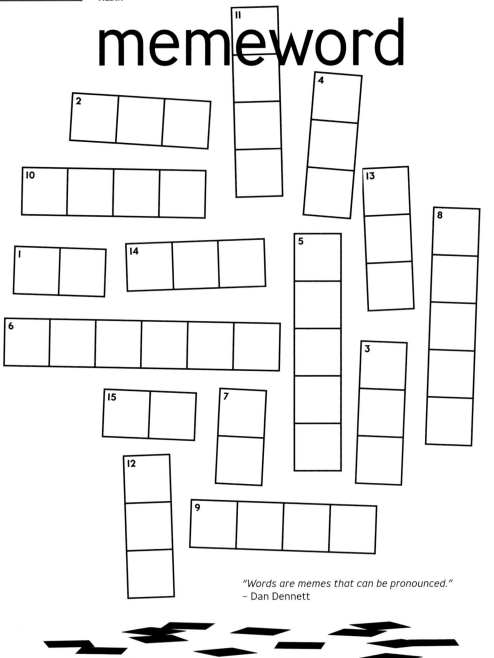

"Words are memes that can be pronounced."
– Dan Dennett

memeworld

matter overmind

"We are seeing the emergence of a global brain."
— Al Gore

In culture, memes link minds – just as neurotransmitters link neurons in the brain. Mind is becoming ever more closely connected to mind, and memes are the neurotransmitters of the emerging suprahuman organism.

If memetic connectivity gives rise to, or perhaps in some way *is* consciousness, through the central nervous system of the internet these emergent 'thoughts of a culture' are now subject to a huge technological amplification.

Memetic networks were generally contained within a 'vessel' of some kind which provided a degree of separation from the wider environment. This separation was often geographic: the unique culture of an island nation, for example. Elsewhere, there is the hierarchy of state, city, district, and domicile – nested spheres of influence, separate yet connected.

The 'vessel' that we are all most familiar with is the *human body;* within its semi-permeable walls we are free to exercise our mental autonomy and develop what we call our *individuality.*

As with any highly interconnected network, whether electronic or biological, memetic signals can travel very far very quickly.

Today, many incompatible cultural ideas, nurtured in age old isolation, each with their own character and history, personality and idiosyncrasies, meet and clash like competing notions in one schizophrenic species-wide 'brain', a memetic distributed network desperately trying to achieve cohesion and seek resolution.

As individuals, perhaps we are all simply notions in an emerging human overmind as it thinks itself into existence.

And if so, what kind of ideas might this suprahuman mind be having?

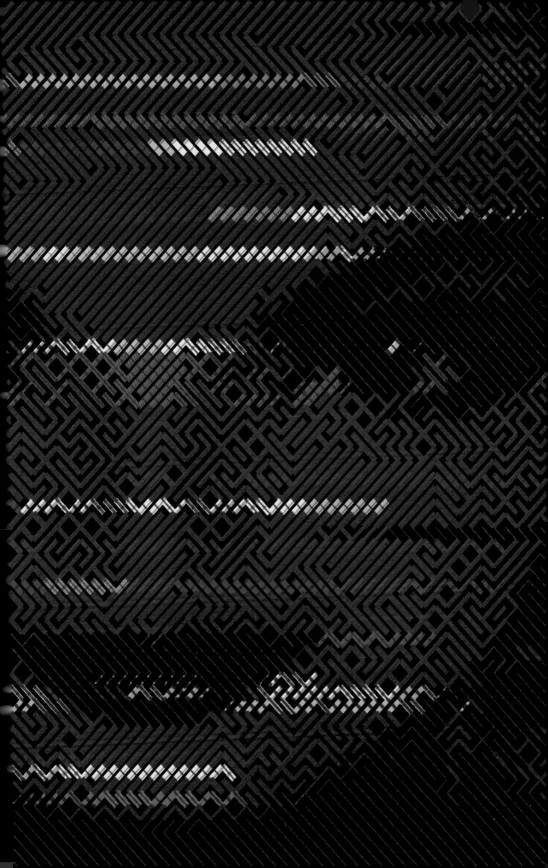

this book has an *idea*

This book is a meme carrier

This book is an Object and a Vessel

REPRESENTATIONS

information content

Images lie on a spectrum, from representational to abstract, particular to universal.

Icons and symbols lie towards the right of the continuum below, whereas more realistic drawings and photographs lie to the left.

What information is lost as we move from left to right? *What do we gain?*

If we extended the sequence further to the left we might next show a film of the house; then offer a guided tour.

Is it possible to take the sequence even further?

What is next in line to the right?

REPRESENTATIONAL
PARTICULAR
DETAILED

**ABSTRACT
UNIVERSAL
SIMPLIFIED**

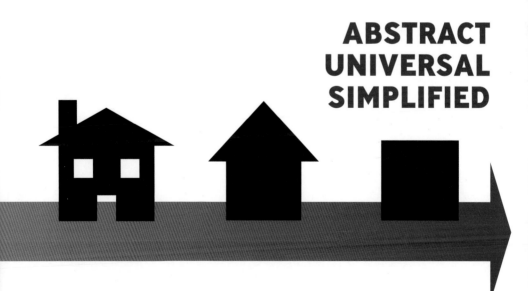

THIS BOOK WAS DESIGNED

Design is purposeful creation.

Design usually involves the structuring of physical objects and thus deals first with *materials* - the substance and method of practical physical expression. *Wood, steel. Ink, paper.*

Design must address the *functionality* of the object - its fitness for purpose.

Aesthetics concerns the visual interrelationships of the *qualities* of these materials - the harmony and relation of colours, shapes, textures; the self-reflective structure. It is a strange mix of 'harmonious universal truths', often considered to be derived from mathematics - the *golden section*, for example – and more representational or culturally derived concerns.

Design is also the structuring of the *meaning* of an object. The success of a piece of design must consider both the practical physical issues and its symbolically or culturally understood meanings - its *message,* what it *says.*

Sign and signified.

Thus, if the basic forms are universal and abstract, the symbolic content is local and particular, and derived first from the anthropological context - simply, from general human experience - and secondly from the relevant cultural context.

The universal, the abstract.

The particular, the specific.

"To redesign a society, one must first redesign the culture."
— Anon

red
square

A shape – a *square.*
A colour – *red.*

A basic geometric shape and a primary colour. Even elements this simple, this elementary, are overlaid with symbolic meanings.

The meaning of *red* is derived first by reference to *nature,* by direct analogy:

Red = *Blood*
Red = *Heat*
Red = *Fire*
Red = *Anger (facial flush)*

Second, by reference to *culture*, by indirect analogy:

Red = *Stop*
Red = *The political left**
Red = *Danger*
Red = *Off*

What about a blue triangle? Or a yellow circle? We have to move to more unusual shapes and colours before any implied meanings begin to lose their grip and shapes and colours become simply just *shapes* and *colours.*

Purple octagon?
Taupe nonagon?
Heliotrope parallelogram?

"Mere colour, unspoiled by meaning, and unallied with definite form, can speak to the soul in a thousand different ways."
— Oscar Wilde

During Mao's Cultural Revolution in China, the Red Guard attempted to reassign the colours of traffic lights so that red signified *go* and green *stop.*

This attempted reassignment of symbols was soon abandoned – *once a meaning has been established, it is very difficult to reassign.*

*In the US and Switzerland, the usual convention of red=leftwing, blue=rightwing is reversed.

10%C, 100%M, 100%Y, 0%BK
R218 G33 B40
L48 a68 b47
H358 S85 B85
Pantone 485M

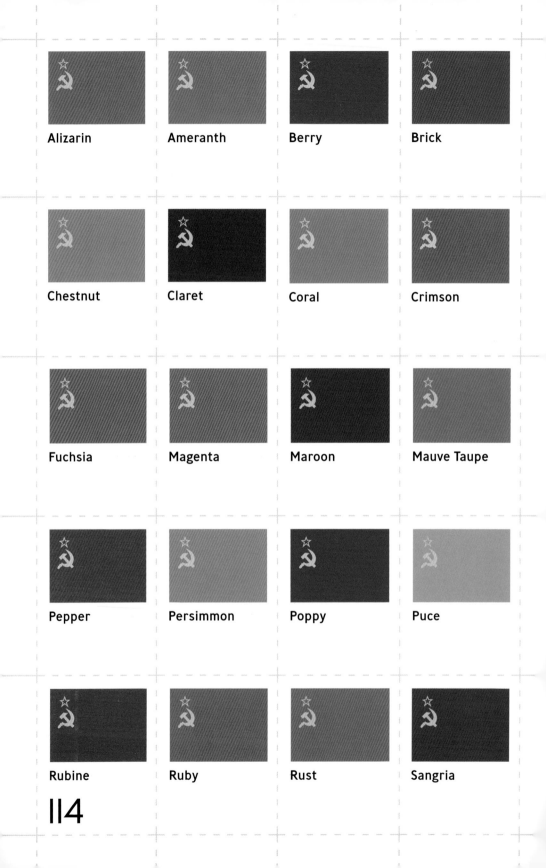

Alizarin

Ameranth

Berry

Brick

Chestnut

Claret

Coral

Crimson

Fuchsia

Magenta

Maroon

Mauve Taupe

Pepper

Persimmon

Poppy

Puce

Rubine

Ruby

Rust

Sangria

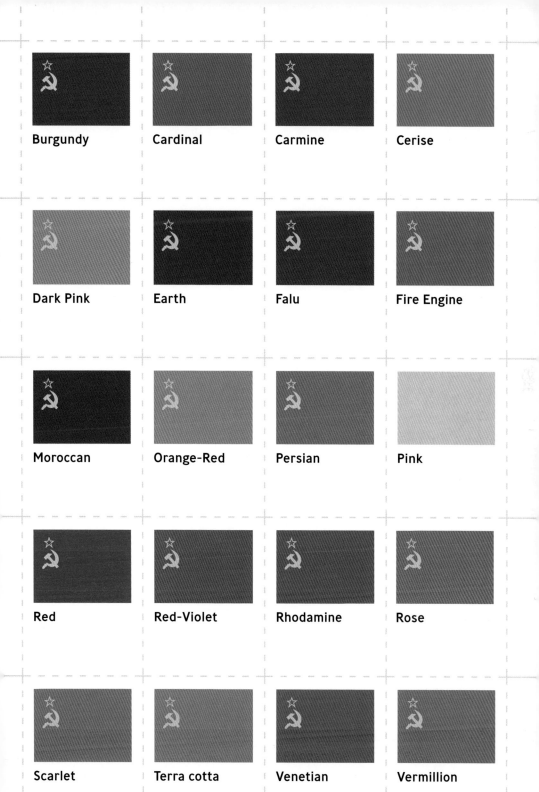

Burgundy

Cardinal

Carmine

Cerise

Dark Pink

Earth

Falu

Fire Engine

Moroccan

Orange-Red

Persian

Pink

Red

Red-Violet

Rhodamine

Rose

Scarlet

Terra cotta

Venetian

Vermillion

brand recognition

And proudly above waves the red, white and blue(s).

Still available:

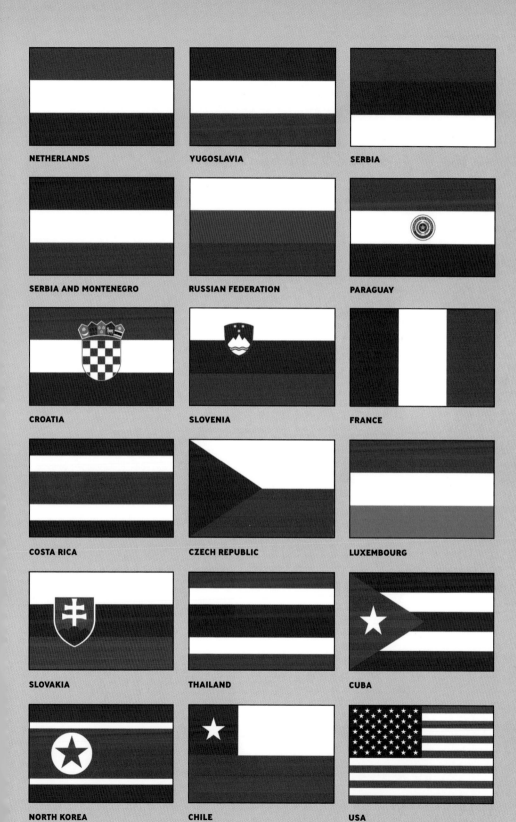

NETHERLANDS

YUGOSLAVIA

SERBIA

SERBIA AND MONTENEGRO

RUSSIAN FEDERATION

PARAGUAY

CROATIA

SLOVENIA

FRANCE

COSTA RICA

CZECH REPUBLIC

LUXEMBOURG

SLOVAKIA

THAILAND

CUBA

NORTH KOREA

CHILE

USA

flags of convenience

If you plan to adopt a flag for your
new republic or political party, you'll
find, like four-letter web addresses,
the simple combinations have already
all been co-opted. Here are some
unused suggestions.

Symbolic readings not included.

COUNTRY A

COUNTRY B

COUNTRY C

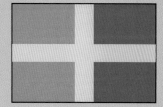

COUNTRY D

COUNTRY E

COUNTRY F

COUNTRY G

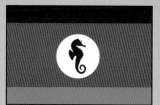

COUNTRY H

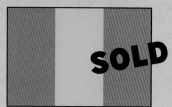

COUNTRY I

COUNTRY J

COUNTRY K

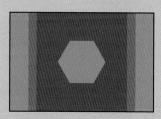

COUNTRY L

COUNTRY M

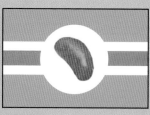

COUNTRY N

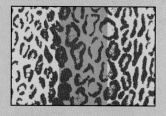

COUNTRY O

COUNTRY P

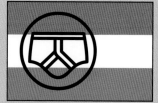

COUNTRY Q

COUNTRY R

talking loud and saying something

Everything we do or make carries meaning - even the simplest clothes we choose to wear still make some kind of statement. It's very hard to say nothing.

"One cannot not communicate."
— Paul Watzlawick

Very little means very little, and meaninglessness is harder to arrive at than might be imagined.

The desire to interpret – and inevitably to *over-interpret* – experience is a powerful one.

"Sometimes a cigar is just a cigar".
— Sigmund Freud

What is the contentless icon, the meaningless symbol, the empty index?

"Are you ready to wear the blank badge?"
— Grant Morrison

Negative space is the space around and between the subject; *the not-subject.*

The art of traditional sculpture consists of removing everything that is not the sculpture.

When Pompeii was being excavated, archaeologists came across numerous empty voids. Pouring plaster into the spaces revealed that they had been left by human and animal bodies: reduced to ashes by the heat, they had survived long enough to leave a negative mould in the cooling lava.

When the surrounding material was removed, expressive figures caught in their dying postures were revealed.

"Thirty spokes unite at the single hub;
It is the empty space which makes the wheel useful.
Mold clay to form a bowl;
It is the empty space which makes the bowl useful.
Cut out windows and doors;
It is the empty space which makes the room useful."
— Lao Tze, *Tao Te Ching*

"Space is the breath of art."
— Frank Lloyd Wright

NEGATIVE SPACE

Above: Ghostly shapes left on a pinboard by the action of the sun
Opposite: Garden of the Fugitives, Pompeii

harmony and beauty tips

Colours, contrary to expectation, are not beautiful or ugly *in and of themselves* - only in *combination*. This suggests that beauty, like harmony, (Greek: *joint, agreement, concord)* is a quality that emerges only as a *relationship* between two or more elements.

Is mud-brown more beautiful than sky blue? If it seems so, it may be because mud-brown is referencing something else in the real world (mud), and the judgement is being made by *analogy* – another form of relationship - and so reflects qualities not inherent in the colour itself.

A single colour is like an isolated pure note: devoid of harmonics, neutral.

"Beauty: the adjustment of all parts proportionately so that one cannot add or subtract or change without impairing the harmony of the whole."
— Leon Battista Alberti

If *ugliness* is a state of antagonistic disharmony, does everything 'ugly' have a counterpoint that would resolve it into beauty - and vice versa?

A dissonant angry work may find a harmonious relationship with a dissonant angry audience. Therein lies its concordant relationship, a mirroring of kind between states.

Could *anything* be seen as beautiful if we could somehow bring ourselves into a harmonious relationship with it?

Beauty, like meaning, resides at the molecular rather than the atomic level - with 'words' rather than 'letters'. These relationships can be temporal or spatial, and the resolving counterpoint that brings consonance and dissonance into balance need not be symmetrical.

Rather than the 'bland perfection of perfect symmetry', balance can be achieved under tension, and resolved off-centre in a dynamic, yet still harmonious *asymmetry.*

'Resolution', in western tonal music theory, is the move of a note or chord from dissonance (an unstable sound) to a consonance (a more final or stable sounding one).

"The creation and destruction of harmonic tensions is essential to the maintenance of compositional drama. Any composition (or improvisation) which remains consistent and 'regular' throughout is, for me, equivalent to watching a movie with only 'good guys' in it."
— Frank Zappa

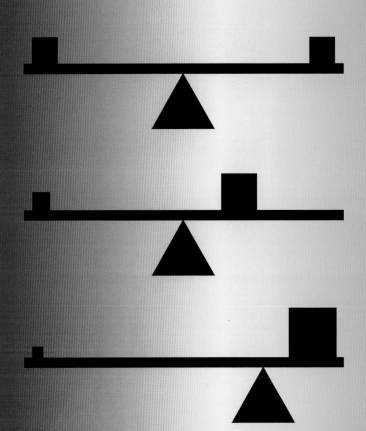

beyond the visible spectrum

All the colours we as humans perceive sit within a narrow band of the *electromagnetic spectrum.* Outside this small visible range lies a territory horizonless and invisible: to one side are microwaves and the infrared, to the other, x-rays and the ultraviolet.

Radio is just a colour we can't see.

Marine mammals have monochrome vision. They are sensitive to light at one wavelength only - they can tell how *bright* it is, but not what *colour.*

Most animals have dichromatic vision. They see the world in two colours, *blue and green.*

Humans have trichromatic vision. The rich diversity of colours we see is made of a mixture of three wavelengths of light: *blue, green and red.*

Birds, however, have four: *blue, green, red and ultraviolet,* They are tetrachromats, living in a four-dimensional colour space.

Compared to these lucky creatures, we are effectively colourblind. How much richer might the world look if we could perceive this extra colour, not only as a fourth primary, but mixing with the familiar colours we know?

2-3% of women may be tetrachromats.

Certain flowers even signal to their potential pollinators using this, to us, unseen part of the spectrum. This invisible ultraviolet colour is known as 'bee purple'.

Flowers come in invisible colours.

Radio
10^3 (wavelength in metres)

Microwave
10^{-2}

Infrared
10^{-5}

130

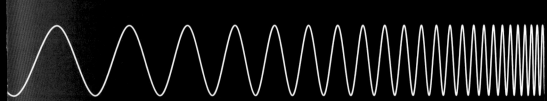

Ultraviolet
10^{-8}

X-Ray
10^{-10}

Gamma Ray
10^{-12}

Above: Mexican 'Creeping' Zinnia *Sanvitalia Procumbens* in visible and ultraviolet light

this is the frame

A frame defines a boundary, a limit.

The frame of a painting tells the viewer: *inside this border is the area the artist exercised control over - this is the extent of the work.* Outside is the area they probably had less control over - *the context, the culture, the rest of the world.*

A frame separates the work from the not-work.

The frame can be seen as a container, not just for a piece of art, but by extension, an idea, an event or a point of view.

A 'framing device' in a novel or film tops and tails the main content.

A 'frame of reference' is the context an object or idea finds itself in; that which does the framing.

Birth and death frame our lives.

A frame, therefore, generally defines a *limit of agency.*

This is my canvas.

inside the frame

. . . is the *work*.

"A painting is a symbol for the universe. Inside it, each piece relates to the other. Each piece is only answerable to the rest of that little world. So, probably in the total universe, there is that kind of total harmony, but we get only little tastes of it."
— Corita Kent

"Art consists of limitation. The most beautiful part of every picture is the frame."
— Gilbert K. Chesterton

outside the frame

... is everything else.

The gallery.
The bookshop.
The social space.
The context.
The *culture*.

window frames

The image contained within the frame can relate to the outside world - *the context, the culture* - in several ways.

It may be directly *representational* - a photograph, or a realistic rendering.

It may be *symbolic,* and describe a non-physical idea, either through pictorial or geometric representation.

It may be *abstract* - the contents of the frame may foreground their 'is-ness', their formal attributes, over their pictorial attributes. In this case, it represents *itself.*

Or it may be a free mix of any or all of the above.

More classical forms tend to foreground the pictorial over the abstract, and subsume the physical qualities of the materials by shaping them into realistic carved and/or painted representations: foliage, finely drawn drapery or the human anatomy.

Other works explore the material's physical qualities and their associated meanings rather than any direct pictorial or representational aspect.

The picture plane can be flattened or fractured; familiar *format conversion* techniques for stepping down 3D reality to 2D representations, such as perspective, can be employed.

A frame can therefore act as a window on a scene and a vessel for an object in itself – *sometimes simultaneously.*

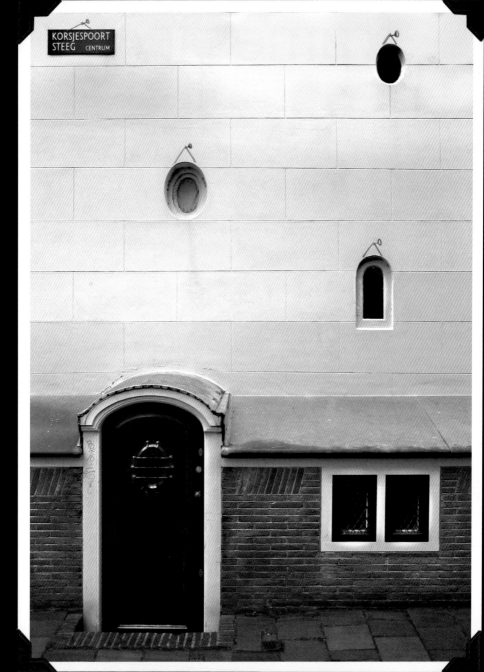

frames in series

A series of frames can have an intentional or accidental inter-relationship; a gallery show in which a number of images are on show, perhaps by the same artist or a selection of artists, for example.

The selection may be formed within the boundaries of another frame - that of an art movement, an *ism;* or possibly the artists are a group of friends, or an overview of work from a specific country. This conceptual frame, the curator's criterion, is used to decide what to include or exclude - what falls on the inside or the outside of the chosen frame.

This will again sit within another frame, the enclosed architectural space of the gallery, the *white cube.*

The white cube itself is framed both within the broader physical location - the city, perhaps - and the critical discourse of the art of the time, which is nested again within certain cultural values and geographical specifics.

And so on out - *frames within frames.*

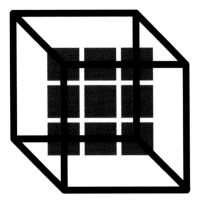

A *sequence of frames* invites the viewer to infer a continuity between them, thus suggesting a time dimension and a narrative. Such is the basis of film, or the language of *le neuvième art,* the comic strip.

Just as perspective is a 3D to 2D format conversion, this sequential ordering serves as a 4D to 2D format conversion.

How to read a comic strip
(West)

How to read a comic strip
(East)

How to travel backwards in time
(West)

How to travel backwards in time
(East)

the frame and where it ends

The edges of a book are a frame – they contain this book. Beyond is your room, the train carriage you're reading this on, the bookshelf or the pulping plant.

In the same way that the gallery frames an artwork, each of these potential environments serve as another frame, a wider context.

Outside this frame there also exist other copies of this book, identical in every way to this one (other than that crease you just put in the spine). They are identical in *form,* but not *location.*

A similar distinction is inherent in the deepest descriptions of matter itself. Subatomic particles are divided into two basic types:

Fermions (particles which adhere to the Pauli Exclusion Principle) can be identical in *form,* but not in *location.* This property means they *occupy space,* and are therefore considered to be the basis of physical matter.

Bosons (particles that obey Bose–Einstein statistics) by contrast can pass through one another unhindered, or happily occupy the same space at the same time – *photons of light,* for example. They are often the particles that *transmit interactions* – the particle equivalent of *memes.*

Connections and connected.

142 WINDOW FRAMES
268 THE BIGGEST FRAME
140 OUTSIDE THE FRAME

frames

within

Frames are not always neatly nested. They overlap, intersect, and can exist within several different contexts simultaneously.

Often one thing can mean two quite different things to different people – or even different things to the same person at different times.

Which frame you are most attuned to
will depend upon your outlook, your
background, your values, your tastes
or your needs.

frames

Culture provides a frame.

the crop and the prop

To *crop* is to impose a frame on a pre-existing situation.

Cropping involves deciding what to include and what to exclude - and what criteria to use for making such a decision.

The *composition* of a photograph, for example, is the organisation of the objects within the frame in a harmonious or conceptually sound manner, in the process excluding elements that may be perceived as inharmonious or irrelevant.

Even a casual and seemingly artless snap has a point of view, a position from which it is observing, and thus involves a choice, a decision.

It is interesting to wonder what may be just out of shot. On a film set, turning the camera 180 degrees would reveal a film studio, a production crew and all the other paraphernalia that making a film requires.

It's akin to lifting the bonnet of a car to reveal the hidden but essential mechanisms at work under the sleek featureless hood.

Pull back, and what more do we see? What didn't make the edit, and why?

The out-takes on the cutting-room floor, the unused shots on the rest of the roll of film, the uncropped original shot – Alberto Korda's iconic photograph of Che Guevara, for example – all can reveal much about the intentions of the editor or the DJ.

Every painting, every photograph, every point of view can be as much about what is omitted as what is included.

maps and frames

A map is a special kind of frame - one in which the interior has a specific informational relationship – *a mapping* – to something exterior.

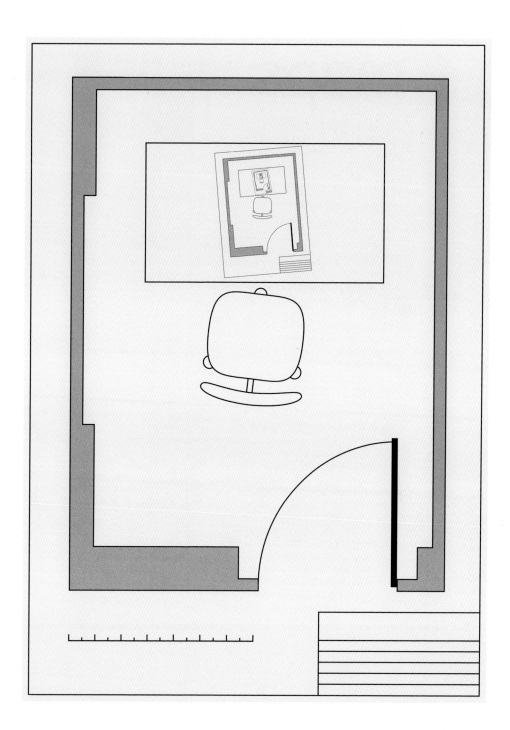

maps

Maps offer a *schematic representation*. They use signs, symbols, codified reproduction, simplification, clarification and omission to represent a *territory*.

Maps can correlate to the territory they map in many ways. Some foreground the physical, some the informational.

It all depends on what is deemed to be important – the *purpose* of the map.

Internally, we build mental maps of the spaces we find ourselves in, both physical and symbolic. We move from the overwhelming complexities of unedited reality to a more streamlined version, where practical utility can trump representational accuracy.

Some maps even depict entirely fictional realms. Like Pooh's Hundred Acre Wood, a fictional construct, by definition, need only be self-reflective (that is *believable*); it does not need to 'map' reality, or to otherwise correspond to it in any way.

The London Underground tube map has evolved from a representational to a more abstract and symbolic – and in some aspects, *fictional* – design.

This latter diagrammatic version, designed by C. C. Beck, has become internalised as Londoner's mental map of their capital city:

"For apparently quite a number of people, the map organized London, rather than London organizing the map."
— Edward Tufte

We gain clarity in one dimension, but lose information deemed extraneous in another.

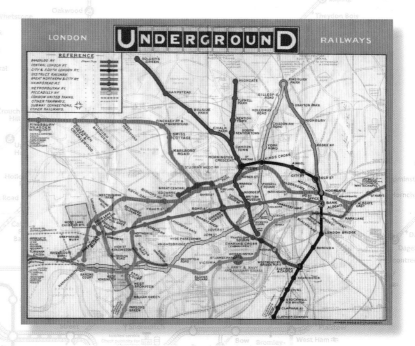

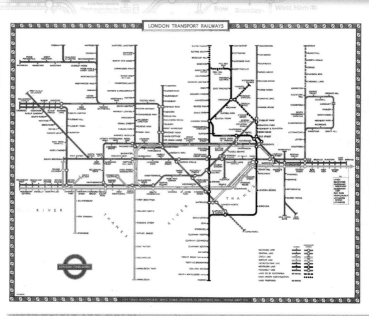

Top: London Underground map, 1908
Bottom: London Underground map, 1951
Background: London Underground map, 2009

© Transport for London
Reproduced by kind permission of
Transport for London

Address:

London
UK

Street view

Get directions - Search nearby
Zoom here - Save to My Maps - Send

A

Address:

London
UK

Street view

Get directions - Search nearby
Zoom here - Save to My Maps - Send

© Google, 2010

culture is a map

Culture is an internalised map, a representation designed to navigate a very particular kind of territory - the local *memeworld*.

Like a physical map, it will have its simplifications, approximations, short cuts, errors and unwanted detail.

And like a physical map, it may or may not reflect reality.

It can have its own idiosyncratic manner of notation, like language; mutually agreed, exclusive.

Each culture will pick out different aspects of the landscape to assign meaning to, and pass silently over others that another culture might deem important.

Culture is a map that makes experience intelligible. It is a map of who, as a whole, we think we are; our values, our art, our intellectual efforts, our gossip, our history.

Learning how to navigate your particular culture, to arrive at your desired destination without getting hopelessly lost, produces a great pressure to comprehend and even conform to the norms of the culture you might happen to find yourself in.

For culture, the map can become the territory.

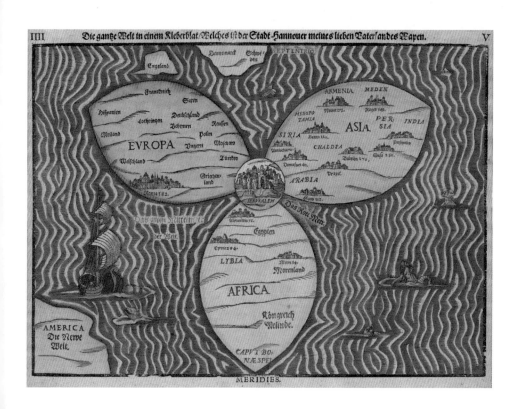

Above: Woodcut map of Jerusalem in relation to the rest of the then-known world, from *Itinerarium Sacrae Scipturae* by Heinrich Bunting, 1545-1606.

this is the map of this book

1: **IDEAS**

2: **COMMUNICATIONS**

3: **MEDIA**

4: **REPRESENTATIONS**

5: **FRAMES AND MAPS**

6: **OBJECTS**

7: **PERCEPTIONS**

8: **SOLUTIONS**

9: **ARTS**

10: **IDENTITIES**

11: **PRESCRIPTIONS**

12: **CODA**

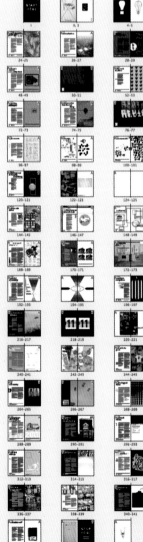

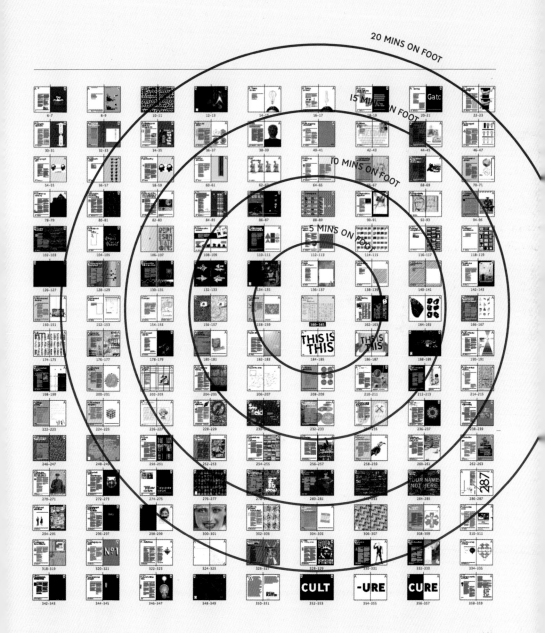

20 MINS ON FOOT

15 MINS ON FOOT

10 MINS ON FOOT

5 MINS ON FOOT

this is the indicia

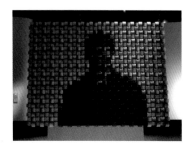

Above: Rian Hughes on Daniel Rozin's 'Weave Mirror', *Decode,* V&A Museum, London, UK 2010

FIELL

Published by
Fiell Publishing Limited
www.fiell.com

Copyright ©2010 Rian Hughes
www.rianhughes.com
©Fiell Publishing Ltd.

All rights reserved.
No part of this publication may be reproduced or transmitted in any form or by any means, electronic or mechanical, including photocopy, recording or any information storage and retrieval system, without prior permission in writing from the publisher.

A catalogue record for this book is available from the British Library.

Standard edition:
US: ISBN 9781906863289
UK: ISBN 9781906863333
Limited edition:
ISBN 9781906863456

Proofreading: Alan Hughes, Maureen Darvell, Peter Fiell

Printed in China

Image credits and locations:

5	IP/BlackJack 3D
7	RH
9	RH
10/11	RH
12/13	RH
15	IP/BlackJack 3D/RH
16	IP/RH
17	IP/RH
18	IP
23	RH
25	Fotosearch/Cueva de las Manos (Cave of the Hands), Santa Cruz, Argentina
27	RH, Texas, Fort Worth, USA
31	Trash icons: Apple Europe
33	RH, Luxor, Egypt
34	RH (top, left), Derek Sadd (right), UK
36	NASA
37	Boy Scout Codewheel, 1931 Burnoy Codemaker, 1934 Phaistos disc: WC, PRA
39	RH/Ben Gilbey
40	Perry Como: Decca Records Sarah Vaughan: Universal Music Publishing Betty Carter: Verve Music
43	RH
45	Bulbs: IP/RH Clive Sinclair, Wigfalls DSJ International Plc.
46	RH
47	BlackJack 3D/RH
50/51	RH
53	RH
55	RH
57	RH
59	RH
61	RH
67	RH, San Diego
62/63	RH
69	RH
71	RH
74	Ultravox: EMI/Midge Ure
75	RH
76/77	RH
78	RH, Limoges, France
79	RH, Cairo, Egypt
80	Columbia Records Catalogue, 1943: Sony UK
82	Mary Jane Darvell/John Hart
83	IP/NASA/RH
84/85	IP/RH
86	RH, Morocco
87	RH
88/89	RH
90	RH
91	IP/RH
92/93	Ron Turner/RH
102	RH
106/107	RH
108	House photo: *Psycho*, 1960 Paramount/Kobal collection
112	RH, Amalfi, Italy
121	RH
122	RH, Pompeii, Italy
123	RH, London, UK
131	©Dr. Klaus Schmitt, Weinheim: www.uvir.eu
132/133	RH, San Diego, USA
134/135	RH, New York, USA
137	IS/RH
143	RH, Amsterdam, Holland
145	RH
147	RH
151	WC/IS/RH
154/155	Harry Beck, after Harry Beck. ©Transport for London, reproduced by kind permission of TFL

156/157	©Google, 2010
159	Heinrich Bunting, 1545-1606
162	Rachel Ainsdale, London
163	RH, London, UK
164/165	RH
167	Fiell collection
169	WC/RH/ Franz Sales Meyer, 1898
170	RH, Hong Kong
171	RH, Kew, London
172/173	RH, Peru
176	RH, Utrecht, Holland
179	RH
181	Lee Stoetzel. Courtesy of Lee Stoetzel/ Mixed Greens Gallery, NYC.
183	RH
186/187	Steven Davis
188/189	RH
190	Board of Governors of Federal Reserve System
196	Ronald C. James, 1966
197	RH
198	RH, London
201	RH
205	RH, Dallas, USA
209	RH
211	NASA
213	R. K. Greville, 1823-1828
215	Myron ©Evan Dorkin
217	RH
218/219	RH
220/221	IP
223	RH
225	IP
227	Johannes Kepler, 1596 *"Aught but Law and Number"* quote from Alan Moore's novel, *Voice of the Fire*
229	William Cunningham, 1559
230/231	NASA/R. Williams/ Hubble Deep Field Team
232	RH
234/235	RH/WC/United States Department of Energy (from Feynman's ID badge) Fox/WC.
237	Thomas the Tank Engine and Friends: ©2009 Gullane (Thomas) Limited
239	RH
241	RH
245	RH, Tywyn, Wales, UK
247	RH, Shenzhen, China
248/249	RH
251	RH, Montreal, Canada
253	RH
255	RH
257	RH
259	Banana: ©The Andy Warhol Foundation for the Visual Arts/Artists Rights Society (ARS), New York/DACS, London 2010/RH
261	RH, Lake Balaton, Hungary
265	WC/Marco Bonavoglia (left), Sqamarabbas (right)
267	Andrew Byrom
268	Jan Tschichold, 1928
270	RH, Prague, former Czechoslovakia
271	Anonymous communist designer/RH
272	Abba: Polar Music International AB
273	RH
274	©Tretchikoff Foundation www.vladimirtretchikoff. com., (left), Leonardo Da Vinci (right)
276/277	RH/Phrenological heads, Science Museum, UK

281	RH
282/283	RH
284/285	RH/BlackJack 3D/IP
289	Popular Mechanics magazine, 1950
291	RH, West Ham, London
294	RH/anonymous artists
297	Calligraphy: Reza Abedini
299	Steve Cook
300/301	Steve Cook
305	IP/Franci
306/307	RH
309	RH
311	May 10 1933 Berlin National Archives and Records Administration /iMac: Apple Europe/RH
312	RH, Paris, France
313	Saron Hughes, London UK
315	RH, Montreal, Canada
317	RH, Ealing, London, UK
319	RH, San Diego, USA
321	RH, Yorkshire, UK
327	RH
328	RH, London
329	RH
330	RH, Kuala Lumpur, Malaysia
331	RH
333	YouTube screenshot: uploaded by username 'IranianRevolution'
334/335	RH
336	RH, New York, USA
337	RH, Puno, Peru (top)/ RH, Hong Kong (bottom)
339	RH, various locations
341	Bomb: Reg White
345	RH
347	RH/Andrew Manley/IP
358	RH
361	RH
362	RH
364	RH

RH	Rian Hughes
IP	istockphoto
WC	Wikipedia Commons

Uncredited diagrams: RH

This book was designed on a 21" iMac 3.06 GHz Intel Core Duo with 4GB 800 MHz DDR2 SDRAM running OS 10.5.8 using Adobe Indesign CS3, Adobe Illustrator CS3, Adobe Photoshop CS3, Fontographer, FontLab and TextEdit. Images were shot on a 10MP Samsung NV24HD camera, a Canon EOS 450D, an iPhone 3G or scanned using an Epson 10000XL scanner. The body text is set in Ministry, a fourteen weight family designed by RH and based on an upper case original by an unknown Ministry of Transport designer, 1933, (updated later by Hubert Llewellyn Smith and J. G. West), stored in the Kew Records Office, Kew Gardens, UK. Available from Device Fonts. Seven proof editions were output at different stages of completion using Lulu Press' Lulu print-to-order service: www.lulu.com.

Every effort has been made to acknowledge copyright holders. Fiell Publishing wish to thank all copyright holders who are included, and apologise for any errors and omissions. If contacted, these will be rectified at the earliest opportunity.

Mixed Sources
Product group from well-managed forests and recycled wood or fibre
www.fsc.org Cert no. XXX-XXX-XXXX
© 1996 Forest Stewardship Council

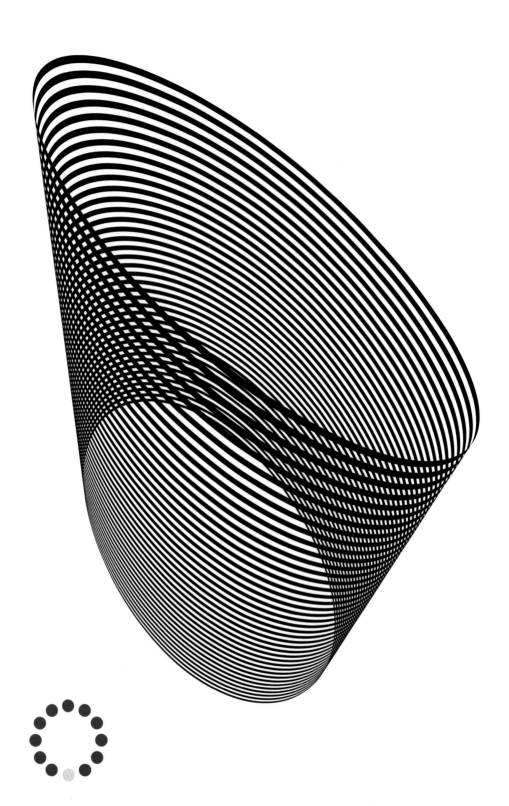

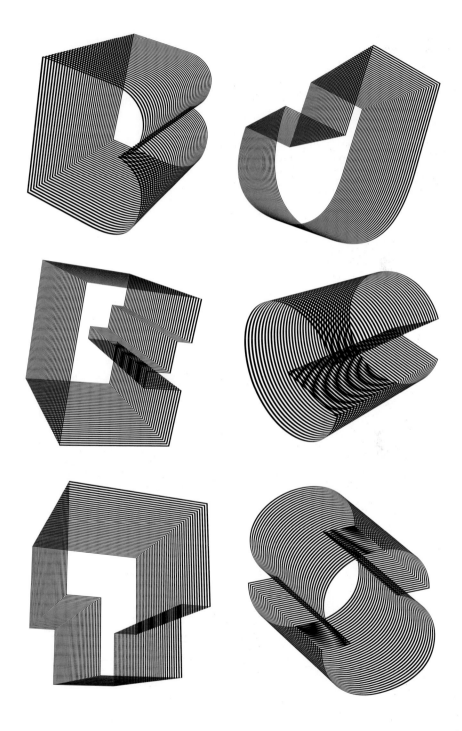

how many times can you solve a problem?

"A throne is only a bench covered with velvet"
— Napoleon Bonaparte

If some problems are difficult to solve, others seem positively fecund with solutions.

The Bauhaus taught that the appearance of a manufactured object should derive from its purpose - that *form follows function.*

Thus it might be assumed that there is one optimal solution to the problem of the chair, and one only; moreover, one that could be arrived at by applying a strict rational formula – and that anything else is *'merely style'.*

But style also has a function.

Style only exists where there is more than one practical solution to a problem.

Style functions not in the practical world of lumbar support, but the aesthetic world of appearance and the cultural world of symbol and meaning.

The *style* of something can be described as beautiful and elegant; it can inform others who we are, display our taste and erudition, our affiliations, our class and our income.

Given that there is not just a single practical solution, the non-practical aspect, the 'art quotient', is free to evolve, to metamorphose; to be subject to creative innovation and the associated cultural cycles of popularity and obscurity that follow.

Style becomes a vibrant form of memetic signalling - a *cultural language*, an *artform*.

As style changes over time it becomes *fashion*. Fashion, like style, can only exist after the practical need, the function, has been fulfilled.

If it ain't broken, fix it.

the crime of ornament

Comprehensive and inarguable, the persuasive power of 'modernism' in the creative arts, especially in architecture, is due to its unbeatable *rationality*.

It is the unquestionable style because it is above and beyond style - it is more akin to a *science*.

Adolf Loos set out the social and architectural aims of the modernist movement in 1908: *"I have made the following discovery and I pass it on to the world: The evolution of culture is synonymous with the removal of ornament from utilitarian objects . . . Lack of ornament is a sign of intellectual power."*

In the age of mass production, ornament, without practical function, is seen as bourgeois affectation, as *bling*.

Modernism attempts to place itself above changeable notions of style or fashion; it draws legitimacy not so much from any inherent aesthetic values but from an appeal to concepts of *universality* and *timelessness*. It widens its 'frame' to also encompass the social, cultural and political.

'Architectural determinism' posited that the design of the spaces we inhabit could improve behaviour and reform society.

This was the utopian social agenda of the modernist architectural movement: *"The character of architectural forms and spaces . . . are powerful agencies in determining the nature of [people's] thoughts, their emotions and their actions."*
— Hugh Ferriss

Romanian dictator Nicolae Ceaucescu enthusiastically put theory into practice with his communist program of 'systematisation'. Small villages were deemed "irrational"; the population was forcibly removed and the old buildings destroyed. Large areas of Bucharest, including historic churches, were bulldozed, and the residents moved into new standardised apartment blocks.

But can modernism itself be a style? The 'exposed frame' of Mies van de Rohe's celebrated modernist icon, the Seagram building, is actually a decorative non-structural concrete cladding. Conversely, so-called 'traditional' architectural forms are often highly evolved practical solutions to the local environment using local materials - the steep, snow-free pitched roof of the Alpine lodge, for example.

If the *appearance* of function does not actually provide functionality, it is essentially an *ideological* or *stylistic* rather than *practical* choice. Beauty does not require ornament, but *ornament can be beautiful.*

Left: The Seagram Building, Mies van der Rohe, 1957
Opposite background: A Handbook of Ornament, Franz Sales Meyer, 1898

cargo cult

What's it worth?

The monetary value of an object is dependent on *position*, both geographically and socially. Moving something from a place where it is common and so has little value to another place where it is rare and thus has a higher value is called *trade*.

Location, location, location.

The *meaning* of the traded item also changes. The same object is placed in different contexts, and acquires different symbolic meanings in each.

Before modern electronic communication, trade was the major vector for the spread of cultural memes.

Couture fashions, for example, were often marketed as being French, even when they came from somewhere else entirely. What they were borrowing (or stealing) was an *association,* a symbolic meaning – in this case one of *exclusivity, sophistication and glamour.*

Not in Paris.

loving the alien

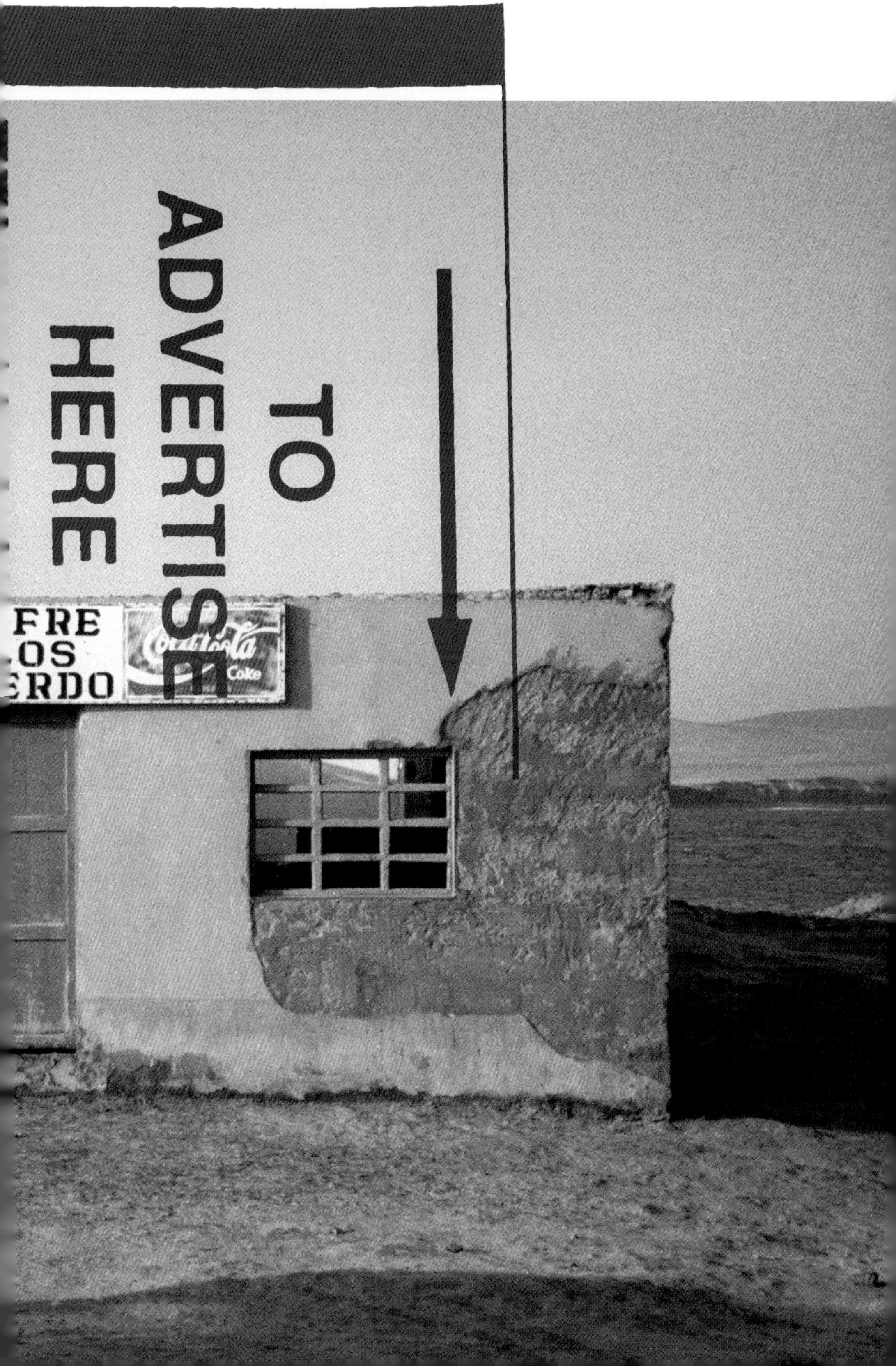
TO
ADVERTISE
HERE
FRE
LOS
ERDO
Coca-Cola
Coke

the meme trade

Packing crate stamps.

CASABLANCA · SUNDBUS · BASLE · COLUMBUS · LUZERN · PARIS · WIEN · GENOVA · LOS ANGELES · BOSTON · GENEVA · HAMBURG · CHICAGO · LE HAVRE

PHILADELPHIA
GENEVA
PARIS
BORDEAUX
CAIRO

ROTTERDAM
NEW YORK
LONG BEACH
PARIS

LOS ANGELES
LONDON
LUZERN
EDMONTON

OSAKA
HAMBURG
GENEVA
HONG KONG
BARCELONA

SINGAPORE
CHICAGO
LONDON
MARSEILLES

temporal position value

The cycle of fashion: *innovation › adoption › saturation › abandonment › reappraisal.*

Cycles upon cycles; innovative revivals and the revival of innovation.

If you're looking for a look, ironic cultural references are *de rigeur* these days, dahling.

Other than a little rust here and some fading there, goods are fixed in their physical *is-ness;* however, their cultural currency changes as the context changes around them.

Unlike the ever-new Now, they sink into the past at the rate of 24 hours a day, seven days a week. They move by standing still. How they are valued and the values they represent change as the objects themselves stay the same.

Yesterday's sale bargains are tomorrow's sought-after collector's items.

The retro look is so next season.

176

SALE Now $24⁹⁵

Sale Bargain

SALE

FINAL

50 off

REDUCTIONS

RTA
.99

Sale SALE

soldes Everything

resonant objects

Objects and phrases can accrue novel symbolic meanings through either purposeful or accidental *association*.

'The Grassy Knoll' is an example of how a resonant meaning is mapped to a word or phrase. This often happens through association with an historical event that becomes a powerful example - *a symbol* - of a certain concept or worldview.

In this case, the meaning maps to a place; in other cases it might map to an object or to a certain time of year.

We may, of course, not be aware of this extra level of meaning – it's possible to explore a museum, for example, and enjoy objects for their purely formal or aesthetic qualities, free from context.

But you can also read the explanatory labels.

Objects, places and times can easily become symbols, loaded with meaning and heavy with significance as they become embedded in their cultural context.

A pair of shoes.

These happen to be Jack Kerouac's shoes.

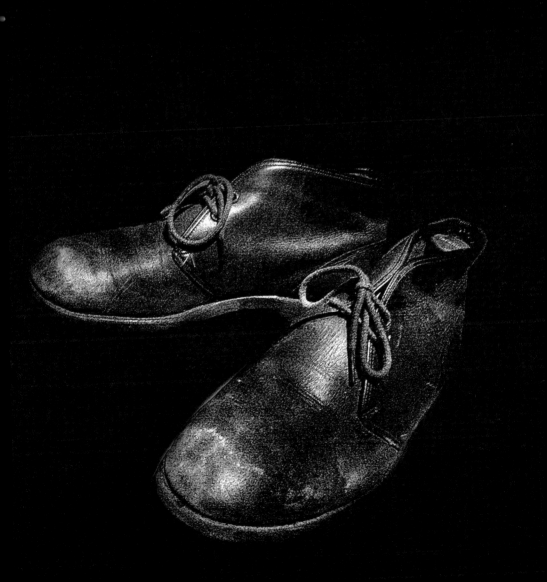

plastic modernism

'Thingness' values the inherent properties of materials for their own sake: *wood grain, stone, cloth, paint.*

Plastic is the modern artificial 'universal medium'. Available in any colour, any shape, any texture, it has no inherent properties of its own, no natural *grain.*

We have developed the pictorial language of the graphical user interface, the tabs, buttons, pages and tools that reference the real world, to enable us to more easily interact and manipulate this abstract realm and bring 'thingness' to a world without real physical extension.

The perfect modernist material. A thing with no thingness.

Pre-plastic, the pliable materials provided by nature such as wood, stone and clay were shaped, carved and painted, the personality of these 'working materials' being purposely subdued in the process.

The *new* perfect plastic material exists in 3D computer space. Infinitely malleable, it can have any shape or quality the designer wishes – except corporeal existence.

It exists purely in the virtual idea-space of a binary description, a space described by mathematics and populated by perfect Platonic shapes. It has no inherent grain, texture, density, taste, smell or shape, *other than that which we choose to ascribe to it.*

is-ness

You could write the most informative review possible of a new record, but being made of words, that review will still not come close to the experience of actually *listening to the song* – what happens when *"the needle hits the vinyl."*

This is another type of *format conversion,* or *media remapping* – a description in one media of something from another. A description, however accurate, is always a step removed, a reinterpretation of the thing itself.

Strangely, though, the *description itself,* now possessed of existence in the real world, has its own unique qualities and, though nothing like the musical experience it describes, is still a *thing* in its own right.

Again, the map becomes territory.

And due to this, can be *mapped itself* - it would be possible to have an article describing the history of the music review - *a review of reviews.* Or a book that detailed the history of mapmaking – *a map of maps.*

Beautifully printed glossy reproductions of photographs of ancient maps in a coffee-table book are representations of representations of representations of representations.

When we ask *"what was it like?"*, we are alluding to this dilemma – being unable to telepathically reproduce experience directly in another's mind, the best descriptions we have rely on comparisons with shared experience. *"You know x? It was just like x. Well kinda. Maybe with a bit of y."*

When we ask:
"What did it feel like?"
"What did it look like?"
"What did it smell like?"

We mean:
What did it *resemble?*

Descriptions mostly rely on *comparisons,* an intricate web of likenesses and differences that, in order to be useful, rely on our being embedded in a common shared experience, a *culture.*

But the fact remains: the most exact description of something is the *thing itself.*

The objectness of the object, the thingness of the thing.

This item has been
temporarily removed

LABEL REORDER REF - ITEM #0223

*"Why is this thus?
What is the reason for
this thusness?"*
— Artemus Ward

184

SIS
SIS

TH
T

"Why is this thus?
What is the reason for
this thusness?"
– Artemus Ward

186

SIS
HIS

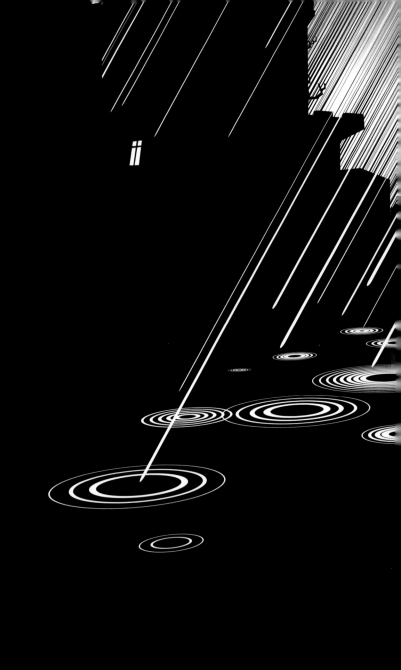

ii

PERCEPTIONS

the 'I' in the pyramid

Where is the 'I'?

Our sense of 'self' is located at the *focus of our attention,* at the point where the *subjective meets the objective* through the senses.

This focal point sits atop an internalised 'processing pyramid', and is the point of entry for the information we receive about the outside world.

Skills once mastered, tricks that have been learned, observations that have been processed are shifted down the pyramid, becoming automated responses that do not need constant re-examination. This frees up the sharp apex of our concentration for the next interesting diversion.

Turning the focus of attention onto these internal processes and away from external sensory inputs is called *reflection.* Or *daydreaming.*

Does all the knowledge we carry come through this 'sharp apex' of experience? Certain skills essential to staying alive seem to be hard-wired in animals at birth. We don't need to learn how to breathe, or be told to eat when we feel hungry.

Certain bodily processes lie on the autonomous borderline. Breathing, for example, can be brought under conscious control when the need arises (and in fact the ability to speak depends upon it), but generally we're happy to delegate that responsibility to our automated systems.

Further down there are processes that we have no conscious knowledge or control over whatsoever – growing our hair, our fingernails, digestion, ageing.

We fade smoothly from the sharp focus of self, down through the animal and into the biological, chemical and mineral.

From 'I' to 'not I'.

"Whatever intelligence is, it can't be intelligence all the way down. It's just dumb stuff at the bottom. Much of biology boils down to chemistry."
— Andy Clark

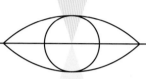

THE FOCUS OF ONE'S ATTENTION ▶

OBJECTIVE, EXTERIOR

SUBJECTIVE, INTERIOR

▲ WITHIN CONSCIOUS CONTROL

OUTSIDE CONSCIOUS CONTROL ▼

DIRECTED CONTROLLED PROCESSES
Learning new skills
and using learned skills in novel ways
Learning a language
Learning how to drive a car
Mastering that Playstation combo move
Learning to play the piano
Executing focussed creative acts

SEMI-AUTONOMOUS PROCESSES
Using learned skills and temporarily
excercising control over normally
autonomous processes
Driving a car
Using that Playstation combo move
Playing the piano
Daydreaming
Holding your breath

FULLY AUTONOMOUS PROCESSES
Processes that function below
conscious control and are primarily
genetic, not memetic
Digestion
Heartbeat
Cell division
Growing your nails and hair
Ageing ......

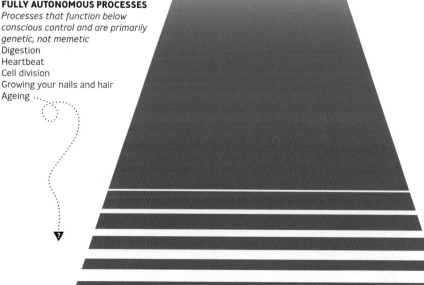

world processing

Scans suggest that the brain produces 'dreams', even during waking hours, but that they are masked by the vivid sensory input of the external world. Dreams are the unfocussed freewheeling of the lower automated processes, left to their own devices while the helmsman at the sharp point of awareness is temporarily out of action.

Outside of our immediate focus, information can still percolate in. Something novel – a sudden movement in our peripheral vision, for example – will be brought instantly to conscious attention, brought into focus. *Is that a predator?*

Our automated processes are busy working for us 24-7, and like employees of a company who for the most part operate unseen, will still drop something on your desk if it needs your urgent attention.

Intuition is the instinctive use of distilled information now residing lower down in the automated processing department – a 'statistical' sum of past experience that provides insights into novel situations.

Another inverted pyramid describes our interaction with the external world, the point of contact located where the seer sees the seen, the hearer hears the heard, the feeler feels the feeling.

This inverted pyramid that extends into the objective world mirrors the subjective one.

First-hand experience is our personal interaction with the external world.

Mediated experience brings within our realm information our senses do not or cannot perceive directly.

Outside that realm, there will be things that will be forever beyond our knowledge and experience.

The extent of our influence in these external realms was originally circumscribed simply by the reach of our voice, the pace of our stride and the stretch of our arm.

This is changing. New media empowers individuals and extends their influence much further. Our 'memetic footprint' has an ever lengthening stride.

Intuition is information coming up from 'below', rather than from 'above'.

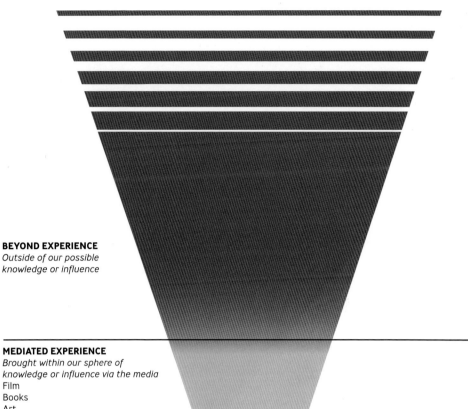

OUTSIDE CONSCIOUS CONTROL ▶

BEYOND EXPERIENCE
*Outside of our possible
knowledge or influence*

MEDIATED EXPERIENCE
*Brought within our sphere of
knowledge or influence via the media*
Film
Books
Art
Gossip
The internet

FIRST-HAND EXPERIENCE
*Within our sphere of direct sense
perception and personal knowledge*
Been there, done that

◀ WITHIN CONSCIOUS CONTROL

THE FOCUS OF ONE'S ATTENTION ▶

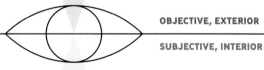

OBJECTIVE, EXTERIOR

SUBJECTIVE, INTERIOR

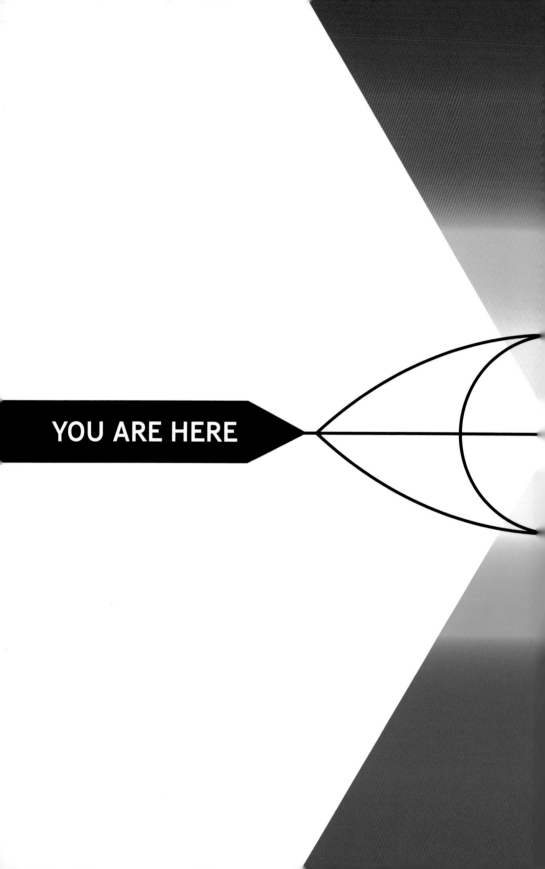

YOU ARE HERE

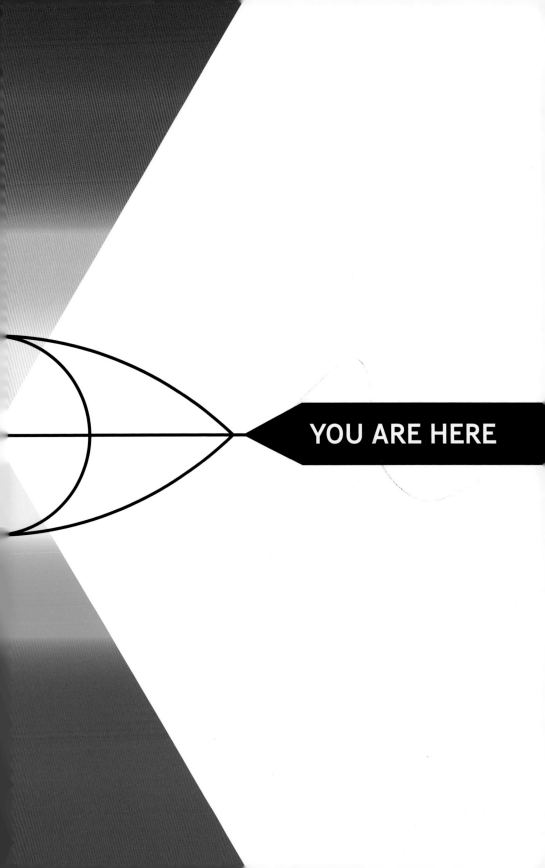

YOU ARE HERE

pattern recognition

The objective exterior world provides the raw material of sensory input.

In order to perceive things clearly, the fidelity of our senses is only half the story, however. This input needs to be *interpreted* - to be internally sifted and processed for *meaning* in the brain.

Upside down, the image to the left is a random collection of splodges. Turn it around, however, and three dimensional forms soon become apparent. The input is essentially the same, but the amount of information we can extract has increased.

We are incredibly sensitive pattern recognition machines.

So efficient is the mind's sensory processing abilities that we are able to build viable maps of the world using a bare minimum of information.

This particularly refined human skill may have evolved because the need to spot a potential predator hidden in tall grass imposes an intense selection pressure.

Maximum output from minimum input. Your life may depend on it.

Above: Photo by Ronald C James, 1966

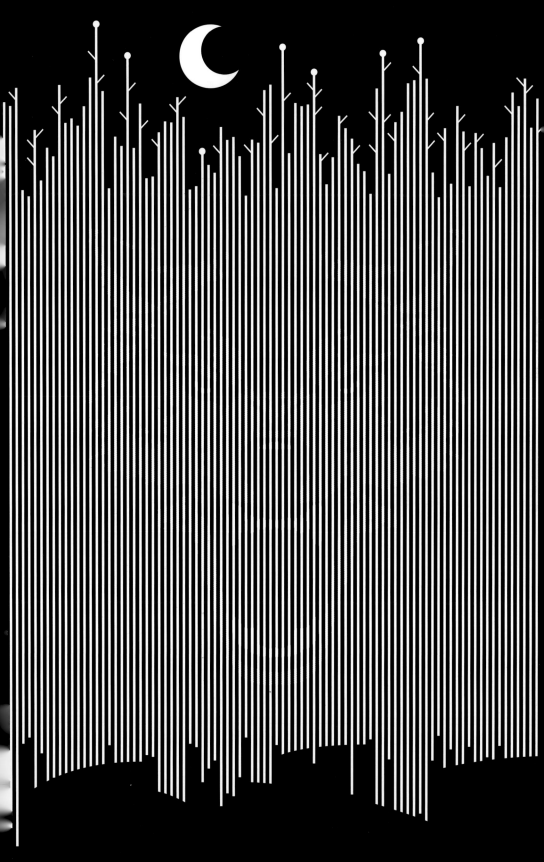

conceptual polyfilla

The brain is so adept at making assumptions about missing information that there are several optical illusions that depend on it.

The *Ehrenstein illusion* (opposite) consists of a grid of lines which terminate a short distance from the points of intersection. The brain will assume that the lines continue, and so perceive the existence of a white circle, brighter than the page background and positioned in front of the intersection, blocking the view.

Conceptual polyfilla.

An analogous effect is achieved by the *Kanizsa Triangle,* an optical illusion first described by the Italian psychologist Gaetano Kanizsa in 1955.

Again, by filling in the gaps in the given information with interpolated assumptions, a complete triangle is seen, even though the contours are discontinuous.

The mind's filling in of the familiar *blind spot*, the part of the eye where the optic nerve exits the retina, is another example.

Gaps in our knowledge, visually and culturally, are bridged with 'intelligent assumptions'.

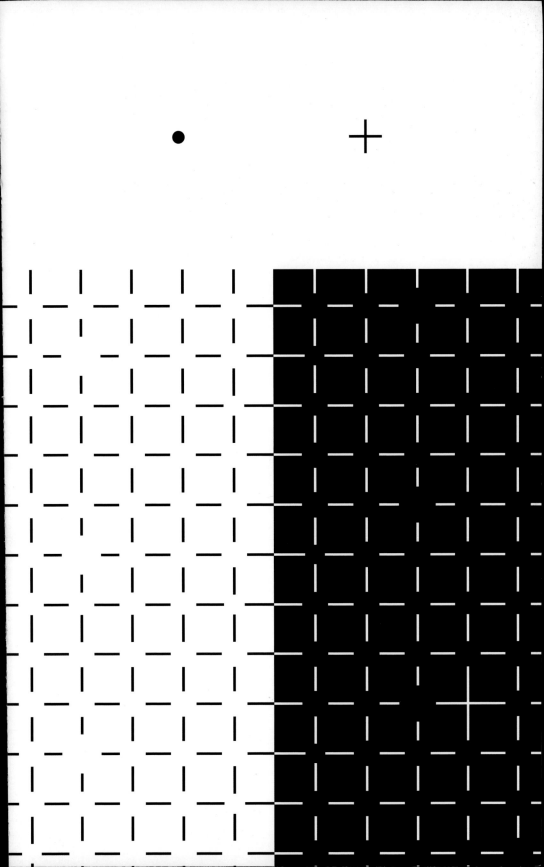

structural intuition

A The ability to see patterns in raw information is called *structural intuition.*

B The mind is hardwired to seek order – *and if none is found, it will tend to impose one.*

The less information we have in a given situation, the more we must be wary of the patterns we deduce from it.

The perceived structure may or may not actually exist.

In survival terms, a 'false positive' is less dangerous than a 'false negative'.

How do we tell them apart? There is a good rule of thumb for sorting valid structural intuitions from invalid ones:

Valid insights are universal.

Every culture, for example, has seen patterns in the stars. Very few, however, have seen the *same* patterns – the constellations differ depending on when and where you are from. The Big Dipper is the Plough in Britain, the Saucepan in France, a stretcher for the sick to the Skidi Pawnee Indians. To the Maya it was a parrot, the Egyptians the leg of a bull. The Hindus interpreted it as the Seven Rishis, or Seven Wise Men, while to the ancient Chinese it was a chariot.

Thus, it is likely that these interpretations are *man-made* creations – local structural intuitions derived from a randomised source – that have no objective reality outside human culture.

If your worldview turns out to only hold locally, chances are it is a cultural construct; your local cuisine as opposed to the study of nutrition, perhaps.

The law of gravity, on the other hand, doesn't change from China to California. We can therefore be reasonably sure we're describing something objective.

This is called the *isotropic principle* – as here, so there.

As above, so below.

200

this is the grid

Many perceived patterns are real.

This is the page layout for this book, the *invisible grid.* The grid gives the information on the page a hierarchy and structure, and extends to every page. Like a solid plot in a novel*, it is an internally consistent artificial creation.*

Explanatory text goes here. The title, in this case 'this is the grid', sits in the top left corner above, and serves as an introduction and summary.

Important points are given emphasis with larger point sizes and *italics.*

This body text is set in 9 on IO point Ministry Light.

The header above, also in Ministry Light, is set in 50 on 42 point.

On the opposite page, an illustration *comments upon, illuminates* or *decorates* the text.

LH#

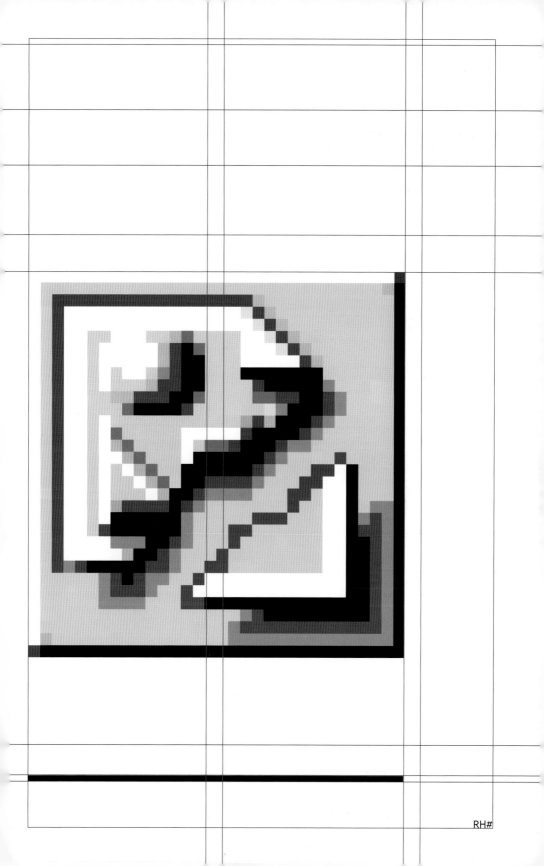

conspiracy theory

The ability to see patterns in images has a *temporal* corollary - the propensity to see causal links in a series of events.

These events may or may not be causally connected in reality.

"When something momentous happens, everything leading up to and away from the event seems momentous too. Even the most trivial detail seems to glow with significance."
— Arthur Goldwag

The *conspiracy theory* is a currently fashionable incarnation of this phenomenon.

Its basic claim – that shadowy powers operate behind the scenes to control world events for their own inscrutable purposes – has striking parallels with the religious worldview, not least in the fact that hard evidence to support either is often hard to come by.

We are all engaged in the continual search for meaning, sifting raw experience and devising mental maps and theories to explain and structure what we perceive.

Several processes can skew our results. *Cognitive bias*, in which evidence that supports a theory is given preferential treatment over evidence that contradicts it is common, as is the avoidance of *cognitive dissonance*, the dislike of simultaneously holding two conflicting ideas.

"If a man is offered a fact which goes against his instincts, he will scrutinize it closely, and unless the evidence is overwhelming, he will refuse to believe it. If, on the other hand, he is offered something which affords a reason for acting in accordance to his instincts, he will accept it even on the slightest evidence.".
— Bertrand Russell

Even so, we can't shake the feeling that momentous events can throw their shadows before them.

We tend to see in natural disasters a displeased deity, in good fortune our just reward.

Are we simply telling ourselves stories, evoking meaning where there is none? How do we differentiate the meaningful from the meaningless?

And is that meaning valid, even if it is just a *personal subjective* meaning?

"Just because you're paranoid, don't mean they're not after you"
— Kurt Cobain

Opposite: Behind the White Picket Fence, the Grassy Knoll, Dallas, USA, October 2004

join the dots

STRUCTURAL INTUITION

GLOBAL WARMING

MICROSOFT

SPIN ICE

BLOODLINE OF JESUS

TROUSERS FOR WOMEN

THULE SOCIETY

NAZI SAUCERS

ELVIS PRESLEY

PAPER MONEY

SETI SMOKESCREEN

WATER FLUORIDATION

BARCODES

DIANA, PRINCESS OF WALES

BOHEMIAN GROVE

ASTROLOGY

CREDIT CHEC

9/11

THE BILDERBERG GROUP

BIBLE CODES

PHANTOM TIME HYPOTHESIS

UFOs

YELLOW

BIG BROTHER

CULT-URE

CULTURE CODES

PLATFORM SHOES

FREEMASONRY

WHITE HEAT SUBJUGATION

THE PHILADELPHIA EXPERIMENT

TRANSFER FEES

WI-FI HEALTH THREAT

THE GUNPOWDER PLOT

NEW WORLD ORDER

FALSE FLAG

THE JOHN BIRCH SOCIETY

SKULL & BONE

FANCIFUL STORYTELLING

CORPORATE TAKEOVERS

FROZEN ENVELOPE THEORY

THE MONTAUK PROJECT

ROCK MUSIC

TELEPORTATION

RONGO-RONGO

THE ORDER OF THE GOLDEN DAWN

THE ILLUMINATI

MARYLIN MONROE'S 6TH TOE

EPISTEMIC BIAS

ALIEN ABDUCTION

MIND CONTROL • AREA 51

APOLLO MOON LANDINGS

REMOTE VIEWING • MEN IN BLACK

THE HULA-HOOP

SHAPE-SHIFTING REPTILIAN ALIENS

TWITTER • HIDDEN MESSAGES IN MUSIC

NUMEROLOGICAL COINCIDENCE

URBAN LEGEND • CUSTARD TART THEORY

NARRATIVE SEDUCTION

SOVIET DOUBLE AGENTS

TRILATERAL COMMISSION • ILLUMINATI

THE CLUB OF ROME • SHADOW GOVERNMENT BLACK OPS

GPS EDITING

GOVERNMENT DISINFORMATION

MAXIMUM DENIABILITY

ALTERNATIVE TECHNOLOGY SURPRESSION

MASS HYSTERIA PLATO'S RETREAT

BLACK BUDGET

ABOVE TOP SECRET

POLITICAL CORRUPTION

REALPOLITIK

THE ROSICRUCIANS

CIA AND ACID • COMMUNISM

APOCALYPTIC PROPHECY • WATERGATE

PRIORY OF SION

THE BLACK POPE

ELECTRONIC IDENTITY CARDS

FOMENKO-NOSOVSKY CHRONOLOGY

UNIFIED FIELD THEORY

THE KNIGHTS TEMPLAR

HI-NRG

DTV TRANSITION • M-J 12 • MASS MEDIA

MORAL PANICS

THE LAST JUDGMENT

DEEP COVER

207

random generators

Pick a random information generator, any random information generator.

Shuffled cards
Tea leaves
Bones
Stars
Sticks
Entrails

Whichever one you choose, you can be pretty sure that at some time it has been used for *divination*.

We look for pattern in chaos and see order in random events.

Throw this book over your shoulder. If it lands front cover up, you will meet a tall handsome stranger.

If it lands front cover down, your money problems will soon be over.

If it lands on the spine or another edge, you have a new career as a trapeze artist ahead of you.

If it lands with the pages splayed open and facing down, someone close to you is not to be trusted.

If you throw it out the window, you are not easily swayed by such interpretations.

Whether we interpret the rumblings of a volcano, the flight patterns of geese, or the fluctuations of the stock market, we are searching for a deeper understanding – looking to uncover *meaning,* to reveal the *underlying purpose.*

We seek messages – omens and portents.

208

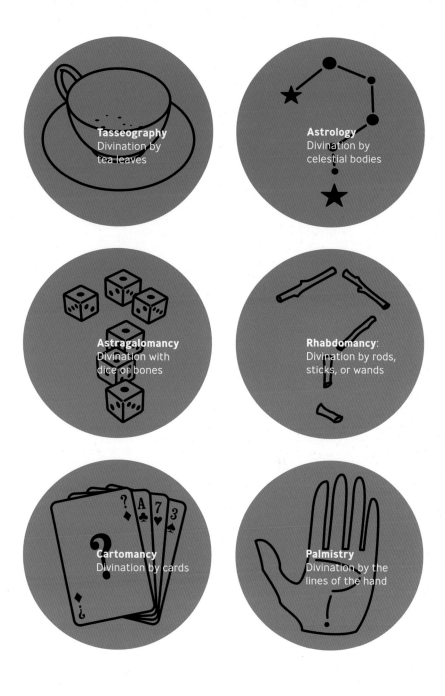

Tasseography
Divination by
tea leaves

Astrology
Divination by
celestial bodies

Astragalomancy
Divination with
dice of bones

Rhabdomancy:
Divination by rods,
sticks, or wands

Cartomancy
Divination by cards

Palmistry
Divination by the
lines of the hand

a beautiful mind

In some people, this pattern-finding ability is so powerful that the perception of false positives – seeing something that just isn't there – has been defined as a medical condition.

Apophenia is the experience of seeing patterns or connections in random or meaningless data. It has been defined as the *"unmotivated seeing of connections"* which can also be accompanied by a *"specific experience of an abnormal meaningfulness"*.

The phenomenon is closely related to autistic spectrum disorders, including Asperger's syndrome. Sometimes called *autistic savants*, these individuals are often aware of *very real* patterns in complex information – numbers or music, for example – that typical observers may miss.

Mathematician John Nash, the subject of the film *A Beautiful Mind*, has this condition. His theories are widely applied today in economics, computing, artificial intelligence and military theory.

Pareidolia is a specific type of apophenia: the perception of images or sounds in random stimuli. Do you ever imagine the phone is ringing while listening to music through headphones or in the shower? Similarly, have you ever seen moving swirls and patterns in television static?

We are especially oversensitive to perceiving human faces in random data.

In fact, there seems to be a specific section of the brain that deals with this socially crucial task. So compartmentalised are some brain functions that injury can impair one's ability to recall a person's name, even while leaving all other perceptions of that person unaltered.

We are made of many parts.

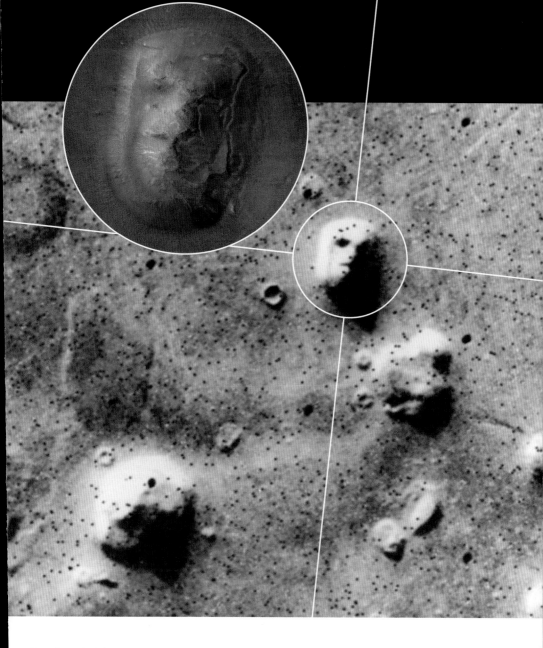

Above: Part of the Cydonia region, taken by the Viking I orbiter and released by NASA/JPL on July 25, 1976, featuring the 'Face on Mars'.

Top: Higher resolution view taken by the Mars Global Surveyor, April 2001

211

the creator's signature

ᕼᕼᕼᕼ

The physical appearance of certain plants – or other naturally occurring phenomena – was once thought to symbolise their potential uses:

"God hath imprinted upon the plants, herbs and flowers, as it were in hieroglyphics, the very signature of their virtues."
— Robert Turner

So snakeroot is an antidote for snake venom; lungwort, bloodroot and wormwood expel intestinal parasites. The holes in the leaves of St John's wort *(Hypericum perforatum)* signified its intended use to heal cuts in the skin, and its head-like shape suggested it could be used for conditions relating to the brain.

This idea has a name: *the Doctrine of Signatures.*

According to this philosophy, the world is primed with hidden codes by a benevolent Creator that are designed to communicate *purpose*; and that these codes can be read by the initiated. Nature is, in effect, assumed to be a *symbolic* language, analogous to any human language.

It is a seductive conflation to assume that the patterns of meaning and symbolism, of morality and justice, that humans have invested in the artificial, man-made constructs of language and culture should also apply to the natural world.

"People say, 'How can you see hummingbirds, roses and orchids and not believe in the Lord's splendour?' But if you're going to look at those things, you should look at other things too . . . An African boy with a parasitic worm boring into his eye. Are you telling me he says 'I understand. God deliberately created a worm that's going to blind me?'"
— David Attenborough

As nature and culture become disentangled, astrology gives way to astronomy, alchemy gives way to chemistry, and religion gives way to philosophy, ethics, cultural history and tribalism.

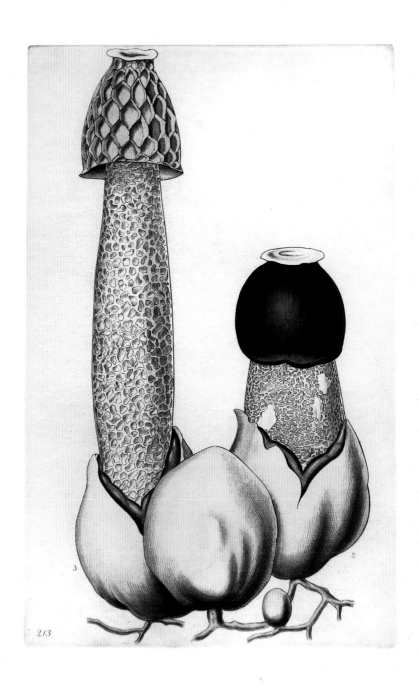

Above: Phallus impudicus (common stinkhorn).
From R. K. Greville's *Scottish Cryptogamic Flora*,
1823 - 1828.

you do that voodoo

Certain traditions hold that an action brought to bear on one object can affect another for which the first is a proxy, without any apparent causal link existing between the two - *that the symbol effectively becomes the symbolised.*

This tendency to perceive a *physical, causal* connection when what is actually being observed is a *symbolic* or *representational* connection is very strong, and is the mechanism through which voodoo is said to operate.

A voodoo doll is an *avatar* - hurt the avatar, hurt the person. The doll may need to have a sample of material from the real-life counterpart to activate the connection - a lock of hair, for example.

The *placebo effect* is a well-documented medical mechanism in which an inert sugar pill is prescribed in lieu of active medication. The patient, unaware of this, nonetheless sees their condition improve.

The opposite effect – where a substance or therapy is implied to be detrimental and thus leads to a patient's deterioration – is called the *nocebo* effect.

Some thoughts can be bad for your health.

Myron, the Living Voodoo Doll by Evan Dorkin

ostentatious ostension

The manufacture of bogus items in support of an idea is both the realm of the hoaxer and the believer.

The hoaxer may do it for amusement, fame, wealth or notoriety – or simply to thumb their nose at the establishment.

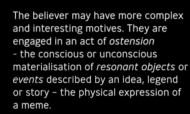

The believer may have more complex and interesting motives. They are engaged in an act of *ostension* - the conscious or unconscious materialisation of *resonant objects* or *events* described by an idea, legend or story – the physical expression of a meme.

These ostentions serve to blur the distinction between the subjective and the objective.

Fact fulfils fiction.

As the power of an idea to spread in a culture is often independent of its truth value, ostentions, like parts of the True Cross, serve as evidence enough for those so inclined.

Can a thought change the physical world?

This is the premise of the placebo effect, prayer – and magic:

"Magick is the Science and Art of causing Change to occur in conformity with Will"
— Aleister Crowley

While the jury is out on the powers of the mind to shape reality in this fashion, in a more practical manner, a thought, strongly held, will affect and guide a person's *actions* – and in this entirely unsupernatural fashion, ideas become actualised in the real world.

"All that I desire to point out is the general principle that life imitates art far more than art imitates life."
— Oscar Wilde

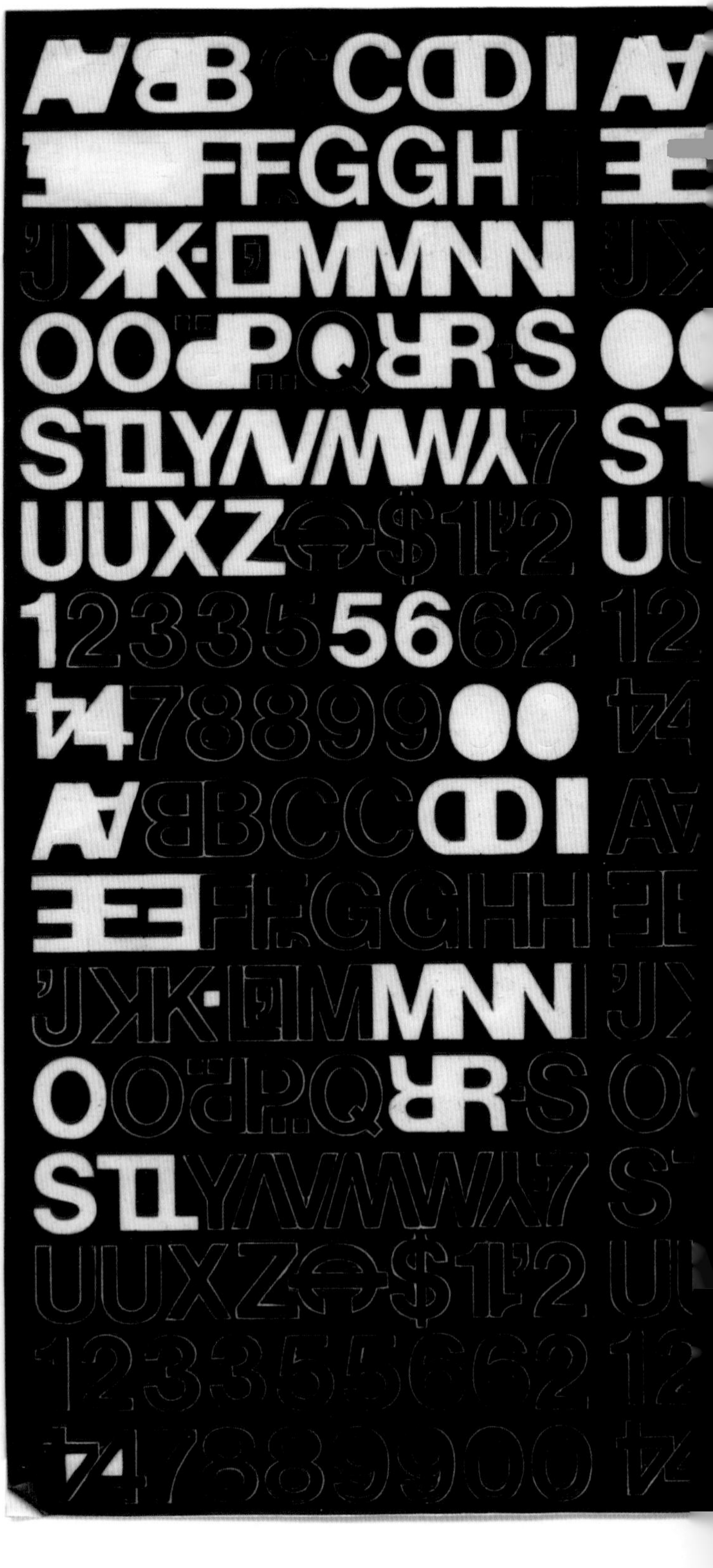

SOLUTIONS

fridge poetry *✳✳✳

Like the 140-character limit on a Twitter 'tweet', constraints, whether practical or intellectual, can paradoxically be a powerful generator of creativity.

"Necessity is the mother of invention" — Plato

Creativity in scientific thought, for example, needs to be consistent with the known facts - or, if it finds itself in disagreement with them, offer a novel reason why.

In the arts, certain poetic forms, such as the haiku or limerick, impose a strict literary format – as does the ordering of the limited number of given words in fridge magnet poetry.

William Burroughs, pioneer of the 'cut-up technique', randomly rearranged words culled from disparate sources, producing unexpected and novel results.

The Surrealists played similar games designed to introduce unusual juxtapositions. Everyday objects, chosen for their familiar, practical, non-symbolic nature - *telephones, cups, irons, lobsters, pipes* - were recast in strange new situations: *"delirious and monstrous amalgamations"* that became the *"point of departure for poetic hallucination"*.

Newly imbued with a numinous quality, these objects could *"open a window on the marvellous that lies hidden behind the everyday."*

But who chooses the original selection?

Who decides the rules of the game?

speak you fool

of naked porcelain angel breath

circle ing his corduroy yesterday s

in the sacred prisoner s warm caramel heart

blush ing some hard marble and concrete rhythm

though stiff from a ferocious translucent steam embrace

then melt and devour their blind dog cake

soft lip s pierce the vast melon perfume d night

of slow cold trust

we said

only

fire like fever

is born or will dance

the rules of the game

Game theory mathematically describes situations where one's choices depend on the choices of others. It assumes a (usually competitive) interaction between players, governed by certain rules.

Game theory has been applied to ethics, politics, economics, biology and social networks, systems where participants evolve common beliefs and useful conventions – a *culture*.

In culture, unlike formal game systems, the rules of the 'game' are open to evolution and change.

All games have rules, and permissible solutions deliver a desired result while elegantly operating *within* these set rules.

A game is said to be 'solved' if it is possible to devise a set of moves to always guarantee a win. Noughts and crosses is one such game. Connect 4 is another. Partially solved games include Chess and Go.

The Rubik's Cube, which could be better described as a puzzle, has an *optimal solution* - a method that produces the final desired state in the least number of moves.

This optimal solution is dubbed 'God's Algorithm'.

It is not known for certain what the minimum number of moves needed to solve any randomly shuffled cube is; currently the estimate is 22.

In the year 333 Alexander the Great attempted to solve the famous Gordian Knot, tied to the shaft of an ox-cart in the palace of the former Kings of Phrygia. It was prophesied that whoever managed this feat would go on to become King of Asia.

Unable to see how the tangle could be undone, Alexander sliced it apart with a stroke of his sword. This became known as the 'Alexandrian Solution'.

It is the ultimate God's Algorithm.

aught but law and number

The very fact that Nature's laws are actually expressible in the form of mathematics has not gone unremarked. Eugene Wigner, in *The Unreasonable Effectiveness of Mathematics in the Natural Sciences* ponders that *"the enormous usefulness of mathematics in the natural sciences is something bordering on the mysterious."*

Many breakthroughs have been made by looking for mathematical correspondences. Just such an insight led James Clerk Maxwell to unify electricity and magnetism: *"The results seem to show that light and magnetism are affections of the same substance; and that light is an electromagnetic disturbance."*

Newton realised that the force that pulls an apple to the ground is the same force that causes the moon to orbit the earth, *"for Nature is very consonant and conformable to herself."*

Of course, 'natural philosophers' also made leaps of inference that turned out to be erroneous. Johannes Kepler proposed that the relative sizes of the orbits of the then-known planets in the Solar System could be described by a nested arrangement of the five Platonic solids. There are exactly five of these solids, which made it hard to accommodate the discovery of a sixth planet, Uranus.

The fact remains: *Nature obeys laws.* They are not an invention of the mind, a cultural construct, or just a convenient model. They are objective and real. They have symmetry and self-similarity across scales and across time.

"Mathematics is the language with which God wrote the universe."
– Galileo Galilei

God's handwriting notwithstanding, Galileo's telescopic observations of the phases of Venus led him to advocate Copernicus' heliocentric (Sun-centred) model of the solar system, which was (and still is) at odds with the geocentric (Earth-centred) Biblical model. His subsequent persecution at the hands of the Catholic Church marks the first great disagreement of fact and faith, observational evidence and traditional authority.

In 1633 he was found guilty of heresy - of holding a view *"as probable, after it has been declared and defined to be contrary to Holy Scripture"*.

Scripture, of course, need not be consonant and conformable to *Nature*.

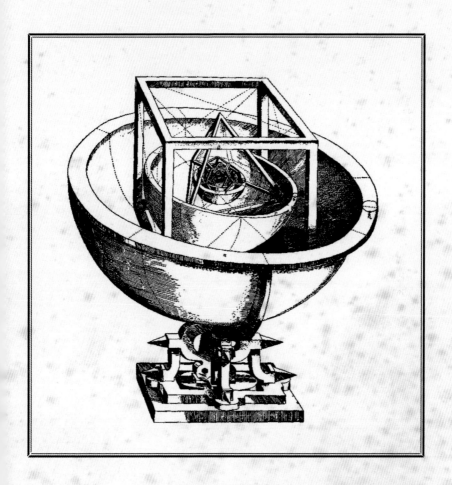

thou wast here

Many societies assumed their horizon encircled the point of creation. At the very centre was the *axis mundi,* the *omphalos* – the 'navel of the world', the universe's place of beginning, the centre of all things. Marked by the spire, the obelisk, the temple mount, it was Dephi, Mount Fuji, Cuzco or Mecca.

The impact of the Copernican revolution – the idea that the planets orbit the Sun, instead of the Sun and planets orbiting the Earth – is this: *the position of the Earth, and thus of mankind, is not privileged.*

We do not occupy the centre of the Universe; in fact, we live in a small backwater of a spiral arm of an average galaxy called the Milky Way.

"Our sun is one of 100 billion stars in our galaxy. Our galaxy is one of billions of galaxies populating the universe. It would be the height of presumption to think that we are the only living things in that enormous immensity."
— Wernher von Braun

Point the most powerful telescope ever built at an apparently empty region of space and leave the lens-cap off for ten days. The resultant image is *The Hubble Deep Field*.

Even seemingly empty space is teeming with galaxies, each containing millions of stars and perhaps tens of millions of planets.

Our human-centred view of the cosmos becomes even more provincial.

How long might it be before we meet aliens? And how 'alien' might alien be? For the first time, our culture as a whole would be thrown into sharp relief. When working from an example of *one*, it's very difficult to step outside for a better view. *You are in the experiment, and the experiment is you.*

History tells us that when two markedly different cultures collide several unavoidable things happen. The more 'advanced' peoples inevitably bring many novel ideas with them; new technology, weapons, food – *and also new diseases.*

The stronger culture will also impose, forcefully or by tacit osmosis, its own *cultural ideas* – its *memes* – and, if it has one, its religion.

Maybe we're the first, or only, intelligent life to arise in our small section of the Universe, which is why we've not met anyone else yet.

Or maybe no-one gives their position away in a forest full of wolves.

Opposite: Illustration from *The Cosmographical Glasse* by William Cunningham, 1559, depicting Ptolemy's geocentric conception of the universe.

Hic canet errantē Lunam, Soli*sq; labores*
Ar&urū*q;;pluuia*sq; hyad.gēinosq; triões

in the deep field

The Arecibo Message ▸ 34

The numbers 1 to 10
Atomic numbers for key elements
Formulas for key DNA bases
The DNA double-helix
The number of nucleotides in DNA
A human being
The height of a human being
Earth's population (in 1974)
The Solar System
The Arecibo telescope
The diameter of the telescope

Background: NASA, R. Williams and The Hubble Deep Field Team (STScI)

As we look out, we look back in time.
Ten billion years ago, light left these
galaxies on its journey to Earth.
We therefore see them as they were
ten billion years ago.

At that time, the Earth had not yet
even begun to form.

You are not here.

starting from the wrong place

There is how stuff is, and there is how we *think* stuff is.

The trick is to come up with a reliable methodology for narrowing the gap.

Jean-Baptiste Lamarck theorised that an organism could acquire new characteristics in its lifetime, and that these could be passed on to its offspring. Being compatible with communist ideology, Stalin championed Lamarck's ideas.

Later, the officially approved theory of environmentally acquired inheritance was that of Trofim Lysenko; opposing theories were formally outlawed in 1948. Soviet scientists who didn't follow orthodoxy were subject to demotion, imprisonment in so-called 'correction camps', and even death.

Lamarck and Lysenko both turned out to be wrong. Of Lysenko, Andrei Sakharov stated: *"He is responsible for the shameful backwardness of Soviet biology, and of genetics in particular."*

Stalin, in arguing for a distinction between 'proletarian' and 'bourgeois' science, had subjugated scientific fact to the class struggle. In North Korea today, a teacher can still accuse a pupil of *"blasphemy against Communism"*.

Richard Feynman, Nobel prize-winning physicist and bongo player, took a different tack: *"Reality must take precedence over public relations, for Nature cannot be fooled."*

Cardinal Ratzinger, later Pope Benedict XVI, quotes philosopher of science Paul Feyerabend: *"The church at the time of Galileo was much more faithful to reason than Galileo himself, and also took into consideration the ethical and social consequences of Galileo's doctrine. Its verdict against Galileo was rational and just."*

In 2009, on theological grounds, he condemned the distribution of condoms to fight AIDS in Africa, stating that *"they aggravate the problem."*

"Religion, at base, is the replacement of logic with faith – and faith is unassailable to reason. As soon as we move a cultural discourse from reason, there is no middle ground, no compromise – because any compromise compromises the very basis of revealed unassailable gospel truth. We are between an irresistible force and an immovable object."
— Richard Dawkins

Lost traveller to local: *"Can you direct me to London?"*
Local: *"Well, If I was you, I wouldn't start from here."*

HOW
WE
THINK
THINGS
ARE

HOW
WE
THINK
THINGS
ARE

HOW
THINGS
ARE

HOW
THINGS
ARE

how to equip your intellectual toolbox

> *"Science (from the Latin scientia, 'knowledge') is a method of finding things out. This method is based on the principle that observation is the judge of whether something is so or not. Observation is the ultimate and final judge of the truth of an idea."*
> — Richard Feynman

Science is not a belief system or an ideology, but a *methodology.*

Science attempts to describe the facts. It is neutral and rigorous. And, unlike other models, it has the advantage of being self-correcting, through a constant process of comparison with the real world, reassessment and re-analysis.

What is a theory? An idea that describes the workings of the world and that has predictive power; a mental model of experience; an explanatory story.

> *"First you guess. Then you compute the consequences. Compare the consequences to experience. If it disagrees with experience, the guess is wrong. In that simple statement is the key to science. It doesn't matter how beautiful your guess is or how smart you are or what your name is. If it disagrees with experience, it's wrong. That's all there is to it."*
> — Richard Feynman

Whatever a story's explanatory lure may be, do not be fooled into thinking that because it is elegant and appealing it must therefore be correct.

> *"Science is a way of trying not to fool yourself. The first principle is that you must not fool yourself, and you are the easiest person to fool."*
> — Richard Feynman, from the lecture *"What is and What Should be the Role of Scientific Culture in Modern Society?"*

234

truth and beauty

Can *beauty* be an indicator of *truth?*

Sian Ede, arts director of the Gulbenkian Foundation, runs projects that bring artists and scientists together. She notes, counterintuitively, that *"contemporary scientists frequently talk about beauty and elegance; artists hardly ever do."*

The *appeal to beauty* has long been used as a deductive, intuitive tool. Its apprehension is linked to the workings of our *structural intuition;* a perception of harmony and balance, of pattern and interrelation.

Einstein, a *"scientist with a deep sense of aesthetics"*, stated that the only physical theories which we are willing to accept are the beautiful ones.

"A theory with mathematical beauty is more likely to be correct than an ugly one that fits some experimental data."
— Paul A.M. Dirac

"Mathematics, rightly viewed, possesses not only truth, but supreme beauty."
— Bertrand Russell

Plato was of the opinion that there is an invisible world of concepts and ideas where beauty, truth and justice remain eternal and unchanging, a world of which our everyday experience is an imperfect reflection.

A postmodern view might ask whether beauty and truth have any objective existence and intrinsic value at all. Is it all simply a matter of taste, of context, of subjective opinion, an entirely artificial cultural invention, a bourgeois affectation?

"'Beauty' is a currency system. It is determined by politics, and in the modern age in the West it is the last, best belief system that keeps male dominance intact."
— Naomi Wolf, *The Beauty Myth*

The puritan distrust of the seductive power of beauty arises from a philosophy that seeks value in austerity. In its seductive appeal to the senses, it is seen as a polluting and worldly evil.

If there is a relationship between beauty and truth, it is in the harmonious chime of mind and nature.

"The universe is built on a plan the profound symmetry of which is somehow present in the inner structure of our intellect."
— Paul Valery

"'Beauty is truth, truth beauty,' – that is all Ye know on earth, and all ye need to know."
— John Keats

Opposite, above: Law in order.
Self-similar, reiterative and generative fractal mathematics, as used in art and nature.

reverse engineering

Reverse engineering is what the US government (or a *black ops* department ten levels above top secret) is alledgedly doing with Roswell's crashed flying saucer at Area 51 in the Nevada Desert.

Alien reverse engineering has so far given us the transistor and velcro, if certain sources are to be believed.

The act of doing science – looking at the world and deducing its patterns, and its laws – could be described as the reverse engineering of nature.

The process: a complex data set, culled from observation, is found upon analysis to be describable by a set of simple principles. Sometimes these deduced principles are discovered to be an expression of an even deeper principle; and so on until we arrive at the so-called Theory Of Everything, or TOE for short.

The TOE is not really a Theory Of Everything, however. It does not predict what you ate for breakfast, who will win Big Brother, or the name of your maiden aunt.

Our internal maps of culture develop in the opposite manner to our maps of nature.

They begin with very simplistic binary models - *adults don't know anything, broccoli is evil, Batman is cooler than Superman* - and become more detailed and refined as real-world experience fleshes out these oversimplifications. Clarifications, modifications and exceptions to the rules are added, and the map begins to describe real people in the real world more accurately.

We learn when to use the small fork, what tie to wear to the office, and when burping is inappropriate.

This is called being *cultured.*

Nature's principles are simple and deducible. From complexity we move towards simplicity.

Culture, being a human creation, is as complex and varied as humans themselves. From simplicity, we move towards complexity.

238

mythtaken identity

Myths are theories masquerading as stories; populated with heroes and villains, fact and fiction, history, supposition, retroactive post-rationalisation, cultural assumptions, and most of all the need to find in the sometimes random unfolding of history a *grand narrative.*

Myths are designed to explain both the physical origins of things *and* their meanings. Thus they transmit both history *and* cultural values: morality, justice, prejudice, faith.

Though now disentangled, in some quarters this amalgamation of cultural myth (and the values it communicates) and actual fact continues to this day, albeit clothed in a modern guise.

The Creation Museum, in Petersburg Kentucky, USA, promotes the Christian literalist 'young earth' view. With only 6000-odd years of biblical history to play with, post-rationalist shoehorning lets animatronic vegetarian T-Rexes interact with early humans and occupy cabins on the Ark. A sign at the entrance sets out the museum's remit: *"Prepare to believe."*

Exhibits portray the moral results of a secular worldview: a male teenager views internet pornography while a female teenager discusses having an abortion. The message is clear: believing dinosaurs are around 65 million years old can turn you to the Dark Side.

The acceptance of this conflation of the cultural with the natural and the man-made world of *value* with physical *fact* requires that all 'beliefs', whether secular or faith-based, be seen simply as a matter of personal *choice.* By being inclusive without being discerning, facts become optional extras:

"Dinosaurs . . . every child seems to go through a stage of loving them! We've made our Dinosaurs Learn 'N Folder *to take advantage of this love. Your child will learn about these creatures, where they lived, how we come to know about them, and much more. There is no reference to dates so you are free to insert your family's personal view of the age of the earth and when dinosaurs roamed it".*
— Live and Learn Press, USA

New Scientist magazine ponders: *"We wonder if this approach will catch on with, for example, packs on the Second World War, which invite your family's personal view on which side won it."*

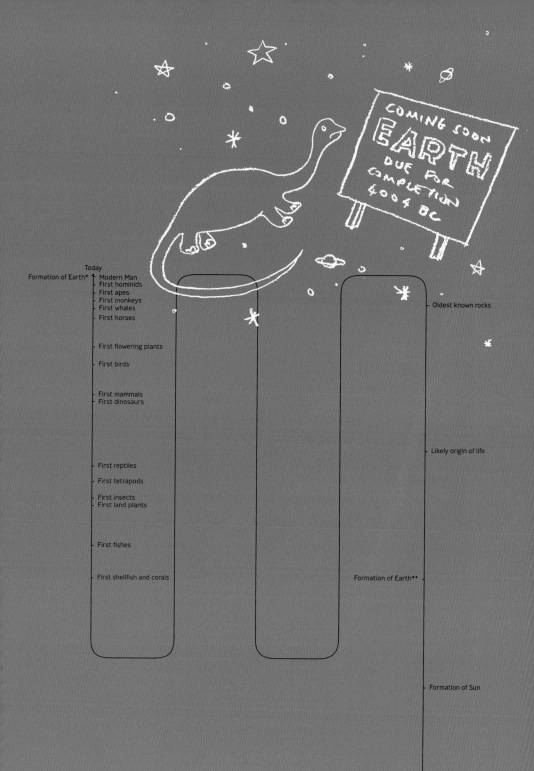

COMING SOON
EARTH
DUE FOR
COMPLETION
4004 BC

Today
Formation of Earth* — Modern Man
- First hominids
- First apes
- First monkeys
- First whales
- First horses

- First flowering plants

- First birds

- First mammals
- First dinosaurs

- First reptiles

- First tetrapods

- First insects
- First land plants

- First fishes

- First shellfish and corals

- Oldest known rocks

- Likely origin of life

Formation of Earth**

- Formation of Sun

* According to scripture
** According to evidence

Likely formation of the Universe - approx 21 feet (640.08 centimeters) this way

philosophies for living

IDEOLOGY #555

IDEOLOGY #45

IDEOLOG #0-0I

IDEOLOGY #556

IDEOLO #HA–

IDEOLOGY #67/9

IDEO #2

LOGY 22

IDEOLOGY #000.23¼

IDEOLOGY #222½

IDEOLOGY #76	IDEOLOGY #77	IDEOLOGY #78	IDEOLOGY #79	IDEOLOGY #80
IDEOLOGY #81	IDEOLOGY #82	IDEOLOGY #83	IDEOLOGY #84	IDEOLOGY #85
IDEOLOGY #86	IDEOLOGY #87	IDEOLOGY #88	IDEOLOGY #89	IDEOLOGY #90
IDEOLOGY #91	IDEOLOGY #92	IDEOLOGY #93	IDEOLOGY #94	IDEOLOGY #95

IDEOLOGY #239

IDEOLOGY #4 (revised)

ALICE

IDEOLOGY #90210 (part 2)

CARLOS

OLOGY #C-1

SANTOS

IDEOLOGY #C-2

NIGEL

IDEOLOGY #X-45

IDEOLOGY #90210 (part 1)

ROVER

IDEOLOGY #7(B)

FRED

IDEOLOGY #X-27

how to be good

"The publication in 1859 of On the Origin of Species . . . demolished a multitude of dogmatic barriers by a single stroke, and aroused a spirit of rebellion against all ancient authorities whose positive and unauthenticated statements were contradicted by modern science."
— Francis Galton

After 150 years, a period which has seen advances in DNA analysis and carbon dating verify and extend the basic concept of evolution beyond all reasonable doubt, the book still serves as a lightning rod.

Many critics point to the lack of an ethical dimension to Darwin's thesis, and imply that we can draw a direct line from it to the policies of Hitler, Stalin and Pol Pot.

Ethical values, of course, are embedded in *culture.* Nature is not only disinterested in such things, it cannot even comprehend them.

"The cosmos is neither moral or immoral; only people are."
— Edward Ericson

Culture, the vessel that carries value and the medium through which it is transmitted, must still conform to fact, and not the other way around: the science behind the atom bomb did not cease to be valid because of the use to which it was put.

How we *use* a technology - whether it be a spearpoint, a gun, a bomb or the internet – *that* is the field of ethics.

A hand, whether raised as a fist or in greeting, is still a hand. What changes is the intent.

Ethics predates organised societies, and even has a counterpart in primate interactions, where an innate appreciation of reciprocal fairness – the so-called 'Golden Rule' – seems to govern group cohesion.

Realising that concepts of ethics are a cultural invention rather than an innate natural law does not in any way devalue their importance. Quite the opposite, in fact – the moral responsibility shouldered by a mature society is the realisation that there isn't any higher justice - there's *just us.*

Ultimately, whether an act is an act of faith or an act of reason, it is still an act, and acts always have consequences.

That is how they are judged.

244

who do you think you are?

"We all remember how many religious wars were fought for a religion of love and gentleness; how many bodies were burned alive with the genuinely kind intention of saving souls from the eternal fire of hell."
— Karl Popper

Despite what Hollywood might suppose, very few people are motivated by what we might call 'evil'. Even tyrants believe they are doing 'good' work, reshaping the world into a better place.

Unless this fact is addressed – that 'good' is a slippery term, one that should only be defined in pragmatic everyday human terms and not by appeal to overarching theologies and ideologies – we will continue to fall prey to virulent memes that promise us 'paradise' but deliver us misery.

Protect me from your best intentions.

Many infectious ideas are powerful because *they contain within themselves the very means of their propagation:* an inherent promotion of absolute values and an encouragement of unthinking obedience.

In this manner a powerful idea can infect a mind so completely that any action, however abhorrent it may be in terms of its human cost, can be justified – and even encouraged.

To see virtue in submitting to the authority of a higher power, to seek absolution in the approval of the pack leader, the alpha-male meme, the overarching idea, is the *acolyte error.*

As Stanley Milgram's famous electroshock experiment demonstrated, *"The disappearance of a sense of responsibility is the most far-reaching consequence of submission to authority."*

"Until we are willing to accept the world the way it is, without miracles that all empirical evidence argues against, without myths that distort our comprehension of nature, we are unlikely to bridge the divide between science and culture and, more importantly, we are unlikely to be fully ready to address the urgent technical challenges facing humanity."
— Lawrence M. Krauss

the pop aesthetic

What is art?

It depends, of course, on who you ask; on whether your criterion is an appeal to structural intuition and beauty, or whether you foreground the *symbolic* significance: *the message, the content, the cultural context.*

"[The nature of art is] one of the most elusive of the traditional problems of human culture."
— Richard Wollheim

Ultimately, your viewpoint depends on where you deem *value* to lie: in sensual enjoyment or ideological relevance, in the sign or the symbolised, the map or the mapped, the label or the labelled – even in the pound or the dollar.

The arts have often been pressed into service by cultural, political, social or religious elites for non-aesthetic ends, to promote certain memes and enforce certain cultural values. When an ideology's grip on the arts finally loosens, *is-ness* tends to reassert itself:

"The avant-garde was dead. Composers wrote tunes again."
— Fiona Maddocks, The Observer

Thus the 'value system' can be top-down – overseen by an elite – or more populist, democratic, and bottom up. Generally it is a messy mix of the two.

What is art?

Vox pop:
"You can tell what it is and it's nice to look at"
— Lisa Adams
Comprehensibility and beauty.

"It's got a beat and you can dance to it."
— Dick Clark, American Bandstand
Self-reflective structure and utility.

'Beauty' and the seductive sheen of craftsmanship, the very *is-ness* of a piece, can be overlooked – not necessarily because it is deemed to be of lesser importance than the symbolic or cultural content, but because it less easily survives the 'media reformatting' into the written and spoken word: *the review, the lecture, the theory.* Beauty is simply harder to describe in language; *sometimes, art is its own best description.*

"The status of an artifact as a work of art results from the ideas a culture applies to it, rather than its inherent physical qualities. Cultural interpretation (an art theory of some kind) is therefore constitutive of an object's arthood."
— Arthur Danto

Theory aside, genuinely popular art, like popular music, simply understands the communicative power of a killer hookline.

251

art?
yeah!

The earliest pigments so far discovered are between 350,000 and 400,000 years old. The oldest known paintings are just 35,000 years old.

The first canvas was the human body, and by decorating it we have continued to create and express our identities ever since we became self-aware.

Pigment could be applied both permanently, as Ötzi the Iceman did in 3300 BC, or temporarily, for hunting, ceremonies and other social rituals.

The 'art' of nomadic or hunter-gatherer peoples had to be portable: decorative clothing, tents, cooking vessels, jewellery and tools. Art could also be *performance,* primarily song and dance. The advent of larger settled communities allowed individuals to develop and hone more specialised skills. Art, of the non-portable and less practical variety, began to flourish.

Thus, for early man, art would represent contemplation over toil. To produce an intricate and beautiful brooch requires *time,* free from the responsibilities of attending to the basic human needs of food, shelter and safety. Art becomes imprinted with the cultural symbolism of a more leisured, refined society – and with the elite who can afford it.

The artistic value of an item can be entirely independent of its functionality. Memes have a sometimes arbitrary relationship to their carrier – the spoken word for example – and the memes carried by art are no different. The concept of the ceremonial sword - ornate, bejewelled, and entirely impractical - epitomises this dual nature.

From a practical standpoint, art is functionally useless – no-one ever died though a lack of song, dance, poetry or sculpture – but from a symbolic and cultural standpoint, it is of the highest significance.

Art, at its most affecting, connects us with the 'sublime', or what some might term the *numinous;* it articulates and makes clear, it can move us and inspire us, it speaks to us and in turn makes us feel understood. It can sometimes seem effortless, because it makes us feel things effortlessly.

In communing with art, we vicariously participate in and, however temporarily, share the artist's expertise in the *objective › subjective › objective* format conversion process.

Art is the song we would sing if we could hold a note, the words we would choose if we were more eloquent, the image we would create if we could just see more clearly.

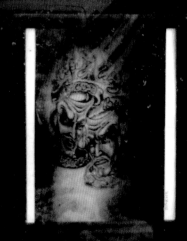

TATTOO

variations on a theme

Variations on a theme are common in the creative arts, especially music.

A set of notes will be repeated throughout a composition, often with minor variations; or flipped, speeded up, slowed down, overlaid and even reversed throughout a piece. Especially popular in Baroque music, Johann Sebastian Bach's *Goldberg Variations* and Beethoven's late variations represent high points of the genre.

Form has a content all its own.

Before exploring the variations, the 'theme' itself first has to be clearly articulated. This is the *baseline*. Creativity (as with a game solution) is often judged relative to some relevant set of criteria - the baseline 'rules'.

These can be real (natural) or artificial (cultural, artistic), depending on whether the subject is a musical theme, a mathematical conundrum or a political logjam.

Any artistic creation also exists in a wider cultural context that forms an extension to the piece itself, an extension which can also be referenced for themes and variations. Thus the subject the particular piece may be referencing may lay outside the piece itself, in the shared history of the form and the creations of others that have come before.

The 'chorus' repeats and evolves through a common culture, through multiple expressions, and embeds itself in and partakes of its time and place.

What is true for ideas in music is true for the ideas that travel through the wider culture. Eventually, if all the possible variations appear to be exhausted, a shift in the original parameters or assumptions can regalvanise a seemingly moribund idea.

The new throws out the assumptions of the old. Yesterday's revolutionaries are today's establishment, and today's revolutionaries will be the establishment of tomorrow.

Repeat to fade . . .

ismism

A generic manifesto template for your own personal movement:

I. We, the Undersigned, have a unique and important Big Idea; an idea that will change the world.

2. We, the Undersigned, will think of a nifty and memorable name for our Big Idea, probably ending in *-ism.*

3. We, the Undersigned, will promote the Big Idea loudly and without compromise, for we believe it is the only valid thing worth doing.

4. We, the Undersigned, will do our best to discourage and discredit opposing views, for they are plainly wrong, and it is obvious at least to us that our Big Idea is the answer to everything from high art to the price of cauliflower.

5. We, the Undersigned, will put people's noses out of joint, but sacrifices must be made, and anyway it is your fault for not understanding the Big Idea because you're either too old, too educated, too bourgeois, too uneducated, too stuck in your ways, too unintelligent, too comfortable, or just don't know what's good for you.

6. We, the Undersigned, will then fall out amongst ourselves due to different interpretations of the Big Idea, and bitter infighting will ensue.

7. We, the Undersigned, will then split up amidst mudslinging and recriminations, go our separate ways, and become part of the group mentioned in Paragraph 5 that the next group of young punks will react against.

Signed:

_____

_____

_____

_____

_____

_____

_____

_____

_____

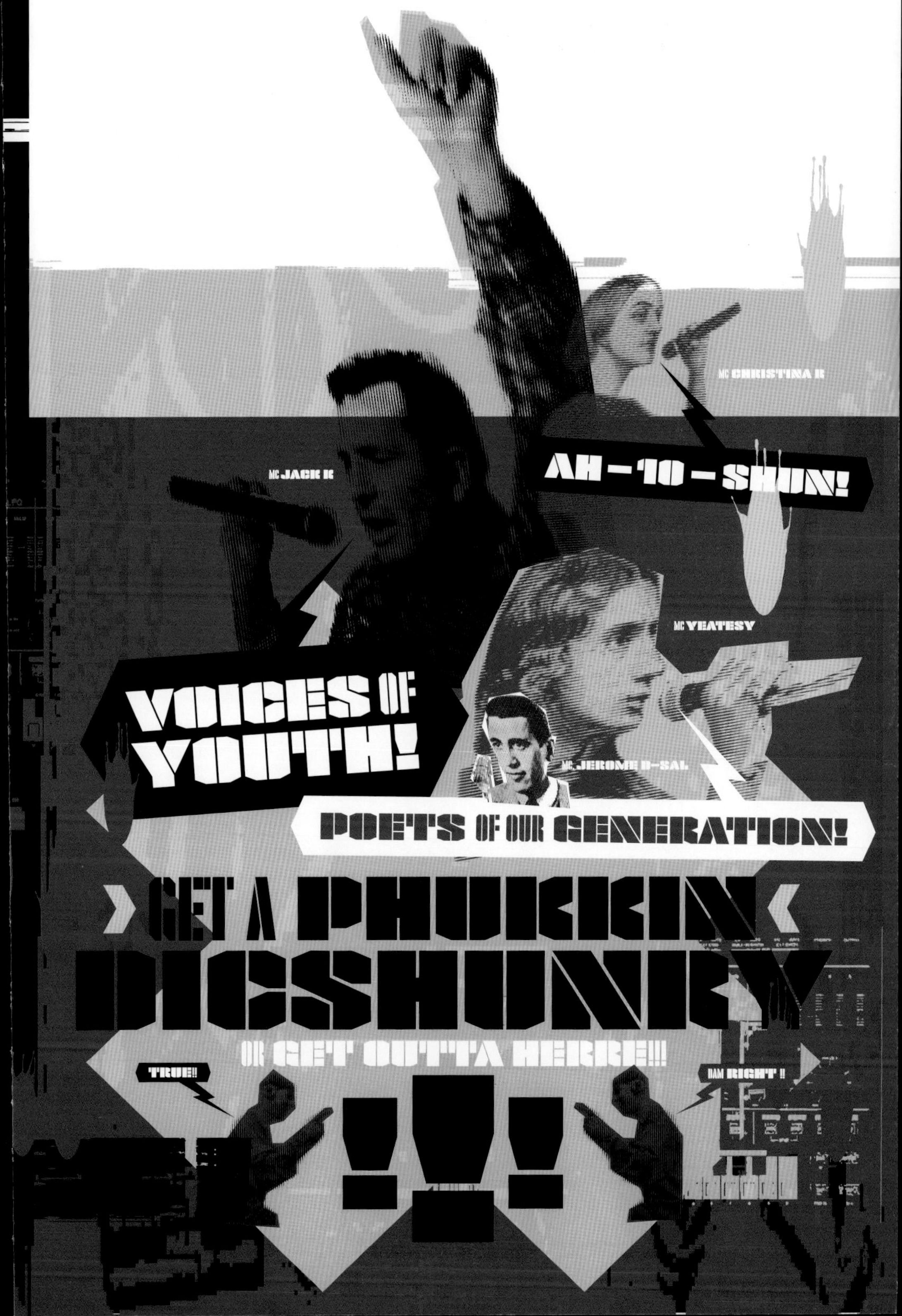
MC CHRISTINA R
MC JACK K
AH – 10 – SHUN!
MC YEATESY
VOICES OF YOUTH!
MC JEROME D-SAL
POETS OF OUR GENERATION!
GET A PHUKKIN DICSHUNRY
OR GET OUTTA HERRE!!!
TRUE!!
DAM RIGHT !!
!!!

warhol passes the baton

The *popular arts* are the classic vectors of youth culture, and youth culture is mainstream culture in the process of becoming, a uniquely sensitive litmus test of the landscape of a nation's psyche - its aspirations, fears and needs, and the direction it's headed.

The popular arts are important as drivers of culture not because the work is necessarily of a high quality (though often it is) but *because the delivery mechanism is so efficient.*

The more efficient the multiplication, the more efficient the dissemination.

If an object is multiplied - a book, for example - it is *democratised.* We can all own a copy. Thus we develop a more personal relationship with the multiplied expressions of popular culture because we experience them in our own private spaces. *We let them into our homes, where they seduce us.*

"The only art movement I knew anything about as a teenager was pop. Pop music is a delivery system that goes straight there . . . into hearts and minds."
— Peter Saville

"Art is the only way to run away without leaving home."
— Twyla Tharp

Warhol, in his appropriation of the multiplied icons of mass produced consumer goods, realised the baton of cultural significance had been passed to the musicians, writers, film-makers, fashion designers, graphic designers, and illustrators - to the artists who operate outside the gallery in the commercial cultural mainstream.

"Art at its most significant is a distant early warning system that can always be relied on to tell the old culture what is beginning to happen to it."
— Marshall McLuhan

The popular arts function as your cultural GPS.

258

sell me a dream, show me a way to be

Popular culture, in the forms of film, TV, music, fashion and art, span the globe, and carry with them the memes of the cultures in which they were created.

For viewers who don't have access to these creative outlets or the lifestyles depicted therein, they can do no less than inspire revolution – or revolutionary hatred.

The Internet, the most efficient meme delivery system yet invented, will soon boast a *"computer in every village in Africa, every school in India"*, and with it will come instant access to the values, lifestyles – and *excesses* – of the developed world.

"As we spread technology, we're the vectors of memes that are correctly viewed by the hosts of many other memes as a dire threat to their favorite memes – the memes that they are prepared to die for."
— Dan Dennett

For many others, it opens up a new frontier of liberating possibilities:

"I have a dream. I go to America, the home of Bruce Springsteen. He write songs for the lonely and the free."
— Spoken to the author by a Hungarian waiter, Lake Balaton, 1991 (right).

"Bruce Springsteen played a gig in East Berlin in July 1988 where he sang Bob Dylan's 'Chimes of Freedom'; some Berliners cite the gig as a pivotal moment. The Wall was a great symbol in pop and rock music. Western pop was brash and decadent, while rock was predicated on notions of freedom; both were effectively banned throughout the stricter, greyer communist world.

"Some have argued that pop music was the battering ram that breached the Wall."
— Kitty Empire, The Observer

From the creative fervour of inarticulate passion that is always youth's fire, make art, not war.

mind the

gap

The culture gap was *generational.*

It described the difference between an older population with more traditional values and a younger population whose new ideas came not primarily from the family or church environment, but from the vibrant, seductive – some may say *dangerous* – 'new media' environment.

The new media of the 50s, 60s was not the internet, but *music, television, film, magazines and comics.*

These are the classic vectors of 'youth culture'.

Unnerved by the possible antisocial influence of these new media – and simply because any new vector that bypasses authority will tend to be perceived as dangerous – the *Senate Subcommittee on Juvenile Delinquency* was set up to investigate. The hearings of spring 1954 focused specifically on comic books:

"I think Hitler was a beginner compared to the comic-book industry".
— testimony of Fredric Wertham, author of *Seduction of the Innocent,* which led to the introduction of the prescriptive Comic Code Authority.

The 'new media' meant that for the first time culture was not primarily being passed *vertically,* from parents to children, but *horizontally.*

Peer-to-peer.

As the world becomes more connected, cultural isolation is becoming rarer – and ever harder to enforce. 'Traditional' and 'modern' cultures, like different generations, are now rubbing shoulders more closely than ever before.

Certain memes that are acceptable in one context will be suspect or even offensive in another: *democracy, free speech, religion, race, the role of women, homosexuality, bacon.*

"These memes are spreading around the world and wiping out whole cultures. They are wiping out languages. They are wiping out traditions."
— Dan Dennett

The Generation Gap has become the Culture Gap.

TEENAGE
TERROR...

ON A
FANTASTIC
RAY-GUN
RAMPAGE!

TEN THOUSAND
TIMES MORE
TERRIFYING...

THAN YOUR
MADDEST
NIGHTMARES...

YOU'LL WATCH
THE WORLD
TREMBLE

IN THE
HORROR-GRIP
OF...

"TEENAGERS FROM OUTER SPACE"

Teenagers from Outer Space, 1959.
The aliens have landed –
and are engaged in memetic war.

pop
idolatry

Iconoclasm: the deliberate destruction of statues, icons, and other symbols or monuments, usually for religious or political motives.

In Christian discourse, iconoclasm is motivated by a strict interpretation of the Ten Commandments, which forbid the making and worshipping of 'graven images'.

Some take a more lenient view:

"I am not of the opinion that through the Gospel all the arts should be banished and driven away, as some zealots want to make us believe; but I wish to see them all, especially music, in the service of Him who gave and created them."
— Martin Luther

In 1975 American jazz-funk fusion band *The Headhunters* took this line of theological philosophy to its natural conclusion: *"God made me funky"*.

A more recent act of iconoclasm was the 2001 destruction of the giant Buddhas of Bamiyan by the Taliban government of Afghanistan. The Taliban banned all forms of imagery, as well as television, music, sport – and the flying of kites – in accordance with their strict interpretation of Islamic sharia law.

Information and Culture Minister Qadratullah Jamal announced the decision, ratified by 400 religious clerics from across Afghanistan, that declared the Buddhist statues which had stood for over 1500 years *"idolatrous and un-Islamic. We are destroying the Buddha statues in accordance with Islamic law and it is purely a religious issue".*

The demolition took several weeks using explosives, anti-aircraft guns, artillery, anti-tank mines and rockets.

The Director General of UNESCO called the demolition of the figures *"a crime against culture".*

The Buddhas of Bamiyan, 507-2001
976

The Buddhas of Bamiyan, 507-2001
2005

No alcohol

No music

No dancing

Hard hat area

Risk of explosion

the biggest frame

Totalitarianism is the imposition of the 'frame', in this case the extent of the ideology's agency, on the culture as a whole – nothing less than the radical reworking of the entire society from the top down. The Biggest Picture.

Everything is part of the canvas, and can be reworked in an attempt to impose a rationality and internal harmony, not just on the *physical* landscape but on the *cultural* one too.

"The Fascist conception of the State is all-embracing; outside of it no human or spiritual values can exist, much less have value. Fascism is totalitarian, and the fascist state - a synthesis and a unit inclusive of all values - interprets, develops, and potentiates the whole life of a people."
— Benito Mussolini

Thus, in the pursuit of an orderly society, the people who make up that society are required to subsume their individual volition to the will of the 'shaper', to bring themselves into a harmonious relationship with the state, the philosophy, the overarching set of memes. An individualistic voice can become a dangerous heresy.

How far can you go to bring order out of chaos, and at what point does imposing order instead become a destructive act?

In the arts, Jan Tschichold, modernist typographer and graphic designer, was well aware that the tenets of modernist design had uncomfortable parallels with social modernism. Both appeal to the 'lust for order', exhibit an inarguable but entirely self-referential logic and offer the all-embracing solution, key features of a totalitarian ideology's seductive allure. Arrested in 1933, ten days into the Nazi regime, for being a *"cultural Bolshevist"*, he managed to escape to Switzerland.

Though still considered a classic, he later described his influential 1928 book *Die Neue Typographie* (The New Typography) as *"too extreme"*, and modernist design in general as being authoritarian and inherently fascistic.

Culture thrives in the gap between chaos and order; too much of either will kill it.

Type ranged left.
Snap to grid.

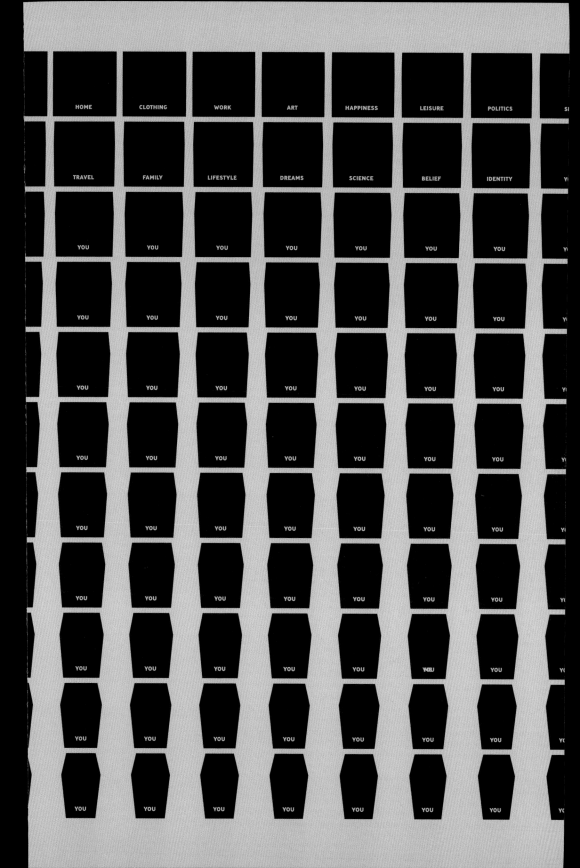

from the factory floor to the dancefloor

Totalitarian movements, whether political or religious, are in the business of *memetic programming*.

In the USSR under communism, anyone wishing to organise a dance would first need to apply for state approval. The event had to be in celebration of a communist-approved theme; the playlist was checked, the lights had to be on at all times.

Culture in North Korea is overseen by the 'Culture and Arts Department of the Central Committee of the Korean Workers' Party'. The 'Mass Games', which involve 100,000 participants in highly synchronised displays with no individual interpretation, present anti-West propaganda and celebrate the Workers' Party Revolution.

"Government by idea tends to take in everything, to make the whole of society obedient to the idea. Spaces not so governed are unconquered, beyond the border, unconverted, a future danger."
— Lord Acton

The tendency is to subsume all aspects of culture into the ideology, regardless of their political or religious content or lack thereof, and to assign those aspects – *art, literature, food, music, science, sex* – even *hats* – a value purely in relation to the ideology.

"Dinner parties were obviously right-wing. Apart from being right-wing in themselves they featured a number of right-wing guest appearances such as wine, suits and mangetouts. And concepts like dessert wine and profiteroles were just off the political scale."
— John O'Farrell

Communism and fascism are two virulent memes that ravaged Europe in the 20th century. These pathogenic ideas infected the minds of several generations before we developed the memetic antibodies to prevent further outbreaks.

Elsewhere, the battle is ongoing. Korea, split at the 38th parallel along ideological grounds, provides a real-world experiment in memetics: divide a uniform population in two, apply a fundamentally different set of ideas to each group, and observe the outcome. Like the division of Berlin, the experiment is blind to race and other biological agencies – it sharply illustrates the impact of just one unique variable: *the application of an idea.*

As viable mainstream ideologies, communism and fascism, in Europe at least, have both been defeated – *for now.*

But where will the *next* contagious and deadly idea come from?

What will be the memetic pandemic of the 21st century?

СЛАВА ВЕЛИКОМУ СТАЛИНУ!

the politics of dancing

380 BC: *"The overseers must be watchful against its insensible corruption . . . against innovations in music and gymnastics counter to the established order . . . for the modes of music are never disturbed without unsettling of the most fundamental political and social conventions."*
— Plato, The Republic

1940: Nazi Germany decreed that works opposed to the regime, or by or about Jewish, African or Marxist subjects, were *"degenerate art" (entartete kunst)*. Modern experimental music was also degenerate, and as for *jazz . . .*

1955: Florida police warn Elvis Presley that if he moves while performing he will be arrested on obscenity charges.

1962: New York's Bishop Burke forbids Catholic school students from dancing The Twist, considering it to be *"lewd and un-Christian."*

2008: *"Rock and disco beats must not be used. [Music] where the dangerous beat plays more of a part than the melody has no place in a society where people are trying to keep their moral standards high."*
— Rabbi Efraim Luft, Committee for Jewish Music

2009: Somalia's Radio Jowhar is closed by the Islamic authorities because it aired *"useless music and love songs for the people . . . we cannot have a radio station playing evil music"*.

"Thank you for the music,
the songs I'm singing
Thanks for all the joy they're bringing
Who can live without it,
I ask in all honesty
What would life be?
Without a song or a dance
what are we?"
— ABBA

"Among the many characteristics which have been identified as peculiar to the human species . . . is the capacity to be delighted and diverted by the exercise of the senses. Even in communities which live on the margins of subsistence, scarce resources of time and energy are dedicated to the pleasures derived from decoration and ornament, and in more developed societies the amount of labour devoted to such provisions is taken to be one of the most significant measures of civilisation."
— Jonathan Miller

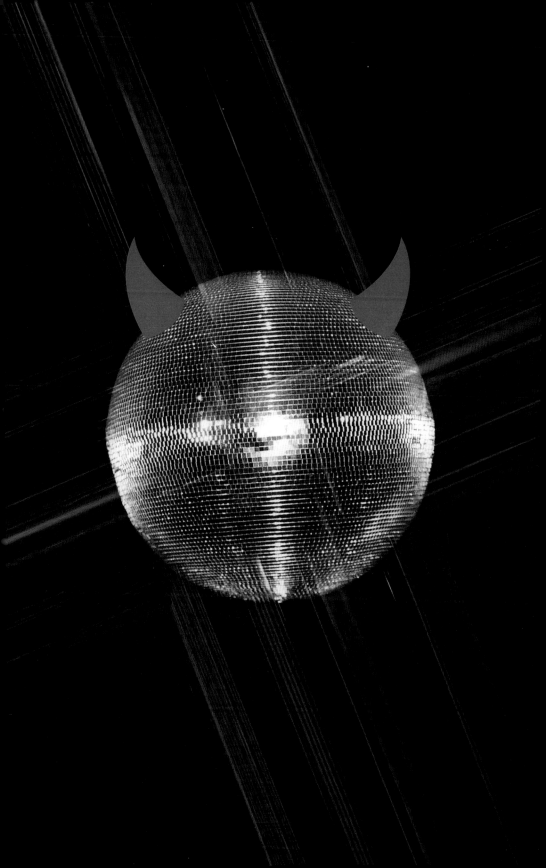

The opposite of

popular culture

Top left: © Tretchikoff Foundation
www.vladimirtretchikoff.com
Top right: Leonardo Da Vinci

is
unpopular culture

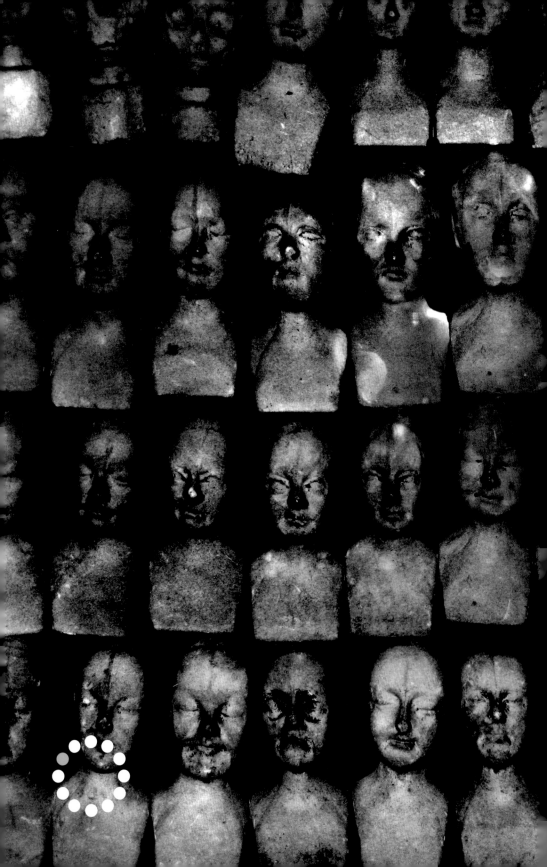

everyone wants to find out how to be

"As an eighteen year old, it was diffi-cult to look at Sean Connery's James Bond and figure out how you were going to do it, because you're not in a casino and you're not going home in an Aston Martin."
— Peter Saville

Learning the Rules of Life, or the norms of behaviour that will get you ahead in your culture, can cause no end of angst, as anyone who has been a teenager finding their way in the world will attest. The 'rules' often seem illogical, complex and contradic-tory. We feel we've not been provided with a manual – the rulebook for life has been left out of the box.

Culture is learned - and we are on a crash course.

Who am I? What's my identity? Where do I fit in? What's it all about?

Choosing an identity is like trying on new suits - we try on several, just to see which fits. Some will turn out to be a step too far, but hey, at least we have the photos to laugh at later. Clothing is an external expression of a process that is going on internally.

We try ideas on for size.

"I can conceive of nothing, in religion, science or philosophy, that is anything more than the proper thing to wear, for a while."
— Charles Hoy Fort

Youth culture inevitably mutates and evolves as each generation remakes it to fit their own image.

Get the exclusive NEW LOOK that everyone's raving about! Now avail-able to all!

Of course, you hope your local idea boutique is well stocked with the lat-est memes, and that, like life for those who grow up far from the bright lights of the big city, the cool stuff isn't all happening elsewhere. Otherwise it's mail-order culture for you.

The global nature of the Internet paradoxically means that there is now even more 'elsewhere', even as it becomes closer to hand.

"And when you want to live, how do you start? Where do you go? Who do you need to know?"
— Morrissey

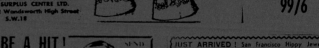

would sir like to try on an idea?

THE OFFICIAL Beatles SWEATER

HIGH FASHIONED BLACK POLO SWEATER IN 100% BOTANY WOOL DESIGNED SPECIALLY FOR BEATLE PEOPLE BY A LEADING BRITISH MANUFACTURER. TOP QUALITY TWO-TONE BEATLE BADGE IS AVAILABLE IN ONE SIZE ONLY. IT IS FASHIONED TO FIT THE WIDEST POSSIBLE RANGE OF AVERAGE-SIZED GIRLS.

SPECIAL OPENING OFFER.

Only 35/-
(Postage and Packing Free!!)

NORMAL MAIL ORDER PRICE 39/11

THE OFFICIAL BEATLES SWEATER INCORPORATING AN EXCLUSIVE AND SPECIALLY DESIGNED TWO-TONE BEATLE BADGE IS AVAILABLE IN ONE SIZE ONLY. IT IS FASHIONED TO FIT THE WIDEST POSSIBLE RANGE OF AVERAGE-SIZED GIRLS.

JET SET JACKETS
BUY BRITISH

B R E A K - THROUGH in price due to increased efficient production.
*Distinctive for men who want a 'cut above' the usual jacket. Smart enough to be worn anywhere, any time.

JET BLACK NYLON with QUILTED GOLD lining or MIDNIGHT BLUE with RED lining. Sizes 34in to 42in

Yours for only **49/11**
plus 3/6d p & p

State Chest Size and Colour Choice
COMMAND SURPLUS CENTRE LTD.
(NME 18), 132 Wandsworth High Street S.W.18

EMBROIDERED FADED LOOK DENIMS
£4.25 + 25p P&P

New flared pants in lightweight faded look blue denim. Ideal for the summer months. Featuring the contrasting, exotic Indian embroidery. When ordering, state waist/hip size

COOL! with this EMBROIDERED SHIRT
This new's day! made poplin with embroidery. Angie's with collar. White, Pink, Green, lilac.

ONLY 99/6

BOYS, BE A HIT!
in this latest BEATLE STYLE JACKET
in popular BLACK CAVALRY TWILL with fancy lining

SEND ONLY 5/- dep.

WONDERFUL BARGAIN **£5.19**
... NOW
AND GET WITH IT!

JUST ARRIVED! San Francisco Hippy Jewellery!
The Polytrend Collection of Beautiful Jewellery for Beautiful People

HIPPY EARRINGS — ONLY **15/6** PAIR
IT'S HERE
HIPPY RING — ONLY **15/-**
HIPPY BRACELET — ONLY **17/6**
HIPPY NECKLACE — ONLY **20/-**
HIPPY BELT — ONLY **23/6**

COMPLETE HIPPY SET **82/6**
ALL POST PAID
POLYTREND LTD.
23 Gt. Titchfield Street, London, W.
(Dept. NME/95)
Trade Enquiries invited

FALSE SIDEBOARDS 'TACHE MOUSTACHE

Send now for these great false sideboards, made in authentic human hair.

PAUL WHITE PRODUCTIONS (Dept. N1), 154 Kenyon Lane, Manchester 10

LEATHER GEAR

WE HAVE EVERYTHING FOR THE ALTERNATIVE GLAMOUR LOOK IN LEATHER, PLASTIC, WET-LOOK, ETC, ETC.

'JACCY-DRESS' £5.00 75/- P/P
JUST SEND £4.00 FOR OUR CATALOGUE (FREE WITH ORDERS) WHOLESALE WELCOME

THE KOOKY SHOP
105 GLOUCESTER ROAD BRIGHTON EAST SUSSEX

SEY BOOTS
'ear' boots—with elastic side gussets. ... seam, rounded toe and 2¼" heel. Hand made, in top quality leather. 5–11, including ½ sizes, also boys, 4½. Colours: black, brown and blue leather; black, brown and navy-blue suede. White and other colours available on request.
75/- per pair, plus 3/- P & P.
Cash with order, or C.O.D. (U.K only). Overseas orders welcome.
45 HERTFORD RD., LONDON, N.9

DONOVAN JACKET
This Donovan Jacket in real suede worn over a turtle neck sweater and hipster slacks, gives a man that "go anywhere, do anything" look. An outfit with a spice of adventure! Jacket in Blue or Sierra Tan Suede 15 gns.

£5.19.6

LEATHER WAISTCOAT
A fun style waistcoat made by finest glove manufacturers in soft supple ... ger brown ... Stud fasten front. Grip with bead chains, or Stonehenge look. 32" bust. Cash with ... Money-back guarantee.

84/-

commodity fetishism

PANTONE®
287C

Fashion is the democratised art of the masses. It is also the most symbol-heavy.

The art of selling aspirational commodities is not simply to sell the product itself, but to imply you also get a glamorous new life to go with it.

Get the shoe/car/watch, get the lifestyle.

This sleight of hand would not work if the audience did not implicitly understand that meaning can be communicated non-verbally, and that *objects can also be symbols*.

Because the connection between the *function* of the actual product and what it *symbolises* can be almost arbitrary, pretty much anything can sport a designer label.

In Western consumer society, the logos and labels designers help create function as modern 'group affiliations', and like old tribal affiliations serve to signal status and exclude the 'other'. 'Exclusive' labels are only exclusive because they exclude - otherwise they'd be 'inclusive designer labels'.

This is not a recent phenomenon. In Greek, Canaan was known as Phoenicia, 'Land of the Purple', because it was the centre of the ancient Tyrian Purple dye industry. Produced from the mucus of certain species of marine molluscs, it took 12,000 of these creatures to produce just 1.5 grams of dye. Only the very wealthy or the aristocracy could afford to wear purple cloth.

Purple implied you were rich, connected, important.

Purple is the original bling.

EXECUTIVE®
gold service

Cour
Club

SILVER
Achievement

Special edition

RITZ

Card Azur™

Platinum™ Clas

classique™
Rendezvous

EXCLUS

Impress® lifestyle awa

International ©

FASHIONED BY
Craftsmen
TO SET THE FASHION

MONACO
style™

RE

label
whores

YOUR

NOT

NAME HERE

Buy my name.
Borrow some glamour.
Because you sure ain't got none,
baby.

Fashion tends to be less prevalent in hierarchical societies, where the style of clothes you wear instead signals status, class, tribe or gender.

Flat cap or top hat, royalty or peasantry, trousers or skirt: you are in uniform, and you are displaying your rank.

In more egalitarian societies we are free to invent our own tribes, with their own dress codes, to belong to.

We can even belong to several at once, a patchwork identity, or none – we could be our own leader, acolyte and follower, a tribe of one.

In a hierarchy, whether it be cultural or on the page of a book, *position* creates meaning.

Size and colour create meaning.

What is important?

What is unimportant?*

Where do we look first?
Order address in do what we the information?

Where are YOU in the hierarchy?

IDENTITIES

1782 hierarchies

*This you can probably skip.

the future ain't what it used to be

Technological change drives social change.

By enabling new modes of interacting, the real impact of the internet, like the printing press and television before it, will be *cultural* - it is primarily a 'soft' technology.

The home of the year 2000, as foreseen in Popular Mechanics magazine, 1950, sees great advances in materials and manufacture, but no change in the role of the housewife.

Many forecasters failed to address social change not because they had a stake in the status quo, but simply because they were embedded in the culture of their times - an unquestionable, unchanging given so unremarkable as to not warrant examination.

Ideas of the future from the past often tell us more about the past than the future.

Forecasters of 1950 could not have foreseen how technology would drive social change. Networking sites, peer-to-peer commerce, blogging and online dating/mating are all changing the way we interact, meet, do business, live and love - *our social culture.*

The only successful prediction we can make about the next 50 years will be that as technology becomes ever more integrated into our lives, our culture will change just as dramatically.

This soft technology will also become invisible. Miniaturisation is only limited by the practicality of the human interface, commonly the keyboard, and if we can find a more direct input method, maybe not even that.

"Any sufficiently advanced technology is indistinguishable from magic."
— Arthur C. Clarke

Because everything in her home is waterproof, the housewife of 2000 can do her daily cleaning with a hose

2000

Above: 'Miracles you'll see in the next 50 years',
Popular Mechanics magazine, 1950.

will the real me please stand up?

Who is the innate you, the real you?

We can't choose our parents, thus we can't choose our race. We can't choose our sex, our height, our eye colour. Thus our first set of affiliations is *genetic* and *compulsory*.

White. Black. French. Chinese. Male. Female. Tall. Short.

Culture is not race. Though born into a culture, our cultural identity is not who we *are* - it is who we are *taught to be.* Our second affiliation is *contingent* and ultimately *optional.* It describes our *memes*, not our genes.

Your memetic identity is not your genetic identity.

Please tick all that apply:

- ■ *Baptist*
- ■ *Trekkie*
- ■ *Genius*
- ■ *Caucasian*
- ■ *Maoist*
- ■ *Platonist*
- ■ *Republican*
- ■ *Human*
- ■ *Other*
- ■ *Vegetarian*
- ■ *Agnostic*
- ■ *Goth*
- ■ *Straight*
- ■ *Disabled*
- ■ *Communist*
- ■ *Gay*
- ■ *Extraterrestrial*

The memes that came with your culture are not immutable, however much they may seem to be that way, because they are *ideas* and not *things.* They are *intellectual,* not *physical* constructs.

And ideas, unlike men, are not created equal.

Although we can choose to be defined by what we believe, what we believe does not have to be defined for us.

Brian:
"Look, you've got it all wrong! You don't need to follow me, you don't need to follow anybody! You've got to think for yourselves! You're all individuals!"
The Crowd:
"Yes! We're all individuals!"
Brian:
"You're all different!"
The Crowd:
"Yes, we are all different!"
Man in Crowd:
"I'm not . . ."
The Crowd: *"Sssh!"*
— Monty Python's *The Life of Brian*

290

▶ 290 YOU'VE GOT TO BE IN IT TO WIN IT
▶ 58 TELEPATHY
▶ 94 EXTEND YOURSELF

default human

You've just loaded *HumanBeing I.0* onto your hardware - your body. Every program comes with a set of factory defaults. What might the defaults for *HumanBeing I.0* be? Probably: *Male. Caucasian. Hetrosexual.* Anything else, and you'll need to customise your preferences.

Our sense of identity includes a long list of our affiliations, the groups we belong to, from the general - *Human Being* - to the specific.

Assume (because often it is assumed) you are a default human – male, Caucasian, heterosexual. You'd need to look much further down the list of options to begin to uniquely describe yourself:

Named Trevor.
Twice-a-week golf player.
Neil Diamond fan.
Handy with a barbecue.
Resident of Essex.

The more egalitarian your culture, the less aspects that make you *different* will affect your opportunities and position – and the freer you will be to explore a more complex, multifaceted and 'customised' individual identity.

The less egalitarian, the more your life options will be restricted by the defaults you happened to be born with. *Poor. Low caste. Female.*

Many ideologies seek to occupy the topmost position in this list of affiliations, to be the *defining aspect* of an individual's identity.

Before you are male, white, or heterosexual – before you are even a *human being,* perhaps – you might be a Christian or a Communist, a Muslim or a Manchester United supporter.

If in order to belong to a group we define ourselves by what makes us *different,* some of us will be considered more different than others. If someone's membership of the group 'Human Being' is lower down the list, and thus less important, than their membership of, say, the 'Aryan Race', where might that lead us?

Only in the face of an overwhelming cultural difference, real or perceived, do we choose to be solely and uniquely defined by what makes us the same, whether that be ideological, cultural or racial – *to tribalise,* rather than celebrate our individuality.

These tribal affiliations can then trump membership of a common humanity, and allow the 'other' to seem less than human.

regional solutions

~~you've got to be in it to win it~~

Who makes a culture?

If you can't   see me

if you can't   hear me

it becomes very difficult for me to contribute to or influence my culture.

The people who *can* participate in a culture are the people who have the opportunity to shape it to their advantage, steer it as they see fit.

If participation is not inclusive, the culture will not be either.

In less egalitarian societies, privilege is conferred by accident of birth. Your class and your sex will define the possible scope of your participation.

If you are male and born into the ruling elite, there is very little incentive for you to change the rules of male entitlement and 'honour': after all, you're just naturally of superior breeding, and so deserve this power, adulation and 'respect', right? That's just how it is.

At the *very* top, there's only The Big Dude above you - and if you happened to be Roman, you could be declared a god and make your way up that last rung anyway, with all the glory and privilege that entailed.

In England, this principle was called the 'Divine Right of Kings', and in China and East Asia the 'Mandate of Heaven'. A monarch was subject to no human law, deriving his right to rule directly from divine authority. All men were *not* created equal.

In more inclusive cultures, those who influence the prevailing values come from a more broadly based sampling of the population.

Politicians, civic leaders, journalists, writers, artists, musicians, businesspeople, actors, bloggers, teachers, game show hosts, reality TV contestants, women . . .

'Respect' tends to be earned, rather than simply being a perk of power and position, class or bloodline – or even simply fear.

Embedded as we are in culture, the medium in which symbols thrive, a *symbolic* separation will thus inevitably create a *physical* separation, and vice versa.

Do you hear me?

customise me

There is a new realm where your gender, class, position or race need not define you.

The digital 'space', built from the ultimate pliable material, is shaped by imagination. In such a space, there are no fixed laws of nature. The strength of gravity, for example, need not be an unchanging one g; it can be tweaked as desired.

Similarly, online avatars – the self-designed embodiment of an online identity – may differ in many ways from the real person they represent.

This is because in designing an avatar it is implicitly understood that the representation is *symbolic;* like the clothes we choose to wear, it communicates our attitudes, interests, tribal affiliations, or sexual availability. In other words, it represents not the outward objective physical appearance of its owner, but their *subjective interior state.* As with any creative act, it externalises the internal. Image *is* meaning, and everyone is a designer.

What is surprising is how robust these new identities can be - and how real they are to the user. Aspirational, expressive, personal and unique, they are unencumbered by the limits of the current real-world plastic surgery and body modification techniques that are available here in the offline universe where the laws of physics are still hard-coded.

We can self-create ourselves.

And there need not just be one of you. Like a wardrobe of identities, each built for a different occasion, you could be someone else tomorrow; or even several people in an evening. We can turn into creatures of our own imagination, not our biological making.

We will all become our own ultimate design project.

Which you is the *realer* you?

who do you want to be today?

NO
PHOTO
YET

A *tulpa*, or thought-form, is a purported being or object which has been created through sheer force of willpower alone: a materialized idea that has taken physical form and moved from the imaginary to the physical. Tradition holds that, while created to serve their master, tulpas can develop their own independence.

As our online avatars begin to perform more of the semi-autonomous processes lower down the processing pyramid for us - information sorting, processing, and other repetitive tasks - could they develop a degree of independent agency?

If, in the performance of these functions, an avatar presents an outsider with a convincing substitute for the real person, how might we tell the difference?

Many artists' 'late periods' consist of regurgitated stylistic ticks with little real innovation. The automatic processes have taken over and the sharp point of attention has become dulled. Perhaps autonomous avatars would mirror this state.

Is this what inevitably happens as we age – novelty becomes disturbing, and our 'comfort zones' shrink to fit?

Even death is no barrier to your continued online existence.

By bequeathing your password, someone else can take over your avatar.

Like the mythical characters of legend that have been rejuvenated and reinvented many times in literature, these characters could become ongoing, even immortal, collaborative efforts.

Choose your successor wisely. Pass on your secret identity, and let someone else assume your cape and cowl.

If it seems that these new entities are not the 'real' ones, consider the fact that they may have been fictions to begin with.

Fiction will bleed into reality – not because, like a tulpa, it achieves actual physical extension, *but because what we perceive as reality will more and more be made of fiction.*

Game never over.

there is power in a name

In *The Nine Billion Names of God*, a short story by Arthur C. Clarke, a group of Buddhist monks attempt to discover His true name. They invent a special writing system which can encode every possibility, and program it into a computer. The monks believe that when the correct name has been found, existence will lose all meaning and the universe will cease to exist. The computer finally finishes the task. Looking up, the protagonist sees *"overhead, without any fuss, the stars were going out"*.

"You can know the name of a bird in all the languages of the world, but when you're finished, you'll know absolutely nothing whatsoever about the bird . . . So let's look at the bird and see what it's doing – that's what counts. I learned very early the difference between knowing the name of something and knowing something."
— Richard Feynman

Surnames originally served as job descriptions: *Thatcher, Smith, Cooper, Baker, Bowman, Fletcher, Tanner.*

Thus, if you knew a person's name, you knew something about them. In some cultures, it is believed that knowledge of a name affords power over the named.

A medical condition, once given a name, will gain a new level of credibility. It can even give the illusion of a deeper understanding or a degree of control, when in fact all we may have is a pattern of symptoms.

A name provides an easily graspable handle that fixes a concept in culture, nails down a new meme, provides us with an identity.

Many cultures have useful words that have no direct equivalent - thus sometimes we borrow, *capishe?*

An *idea without a name* will lose its grip in the competitive memeworld and slip away, leaving people struggling to express it.

Naming is power.

memetic inoculation

During the 15th to the 17th centuries, technological advances in shipbuilding ushered in the Age of Exploration. Previously isolated cultures came into physical contact for the first time.

With these new contacts came new diseases; it is calculated that as much as 90% of the indigenous American population were wiped out by contagions for which they had no immunity. Novel diseases have no compunction about travelling both ways: Swine flu, AIDS and West Nile Virus have more recently been introduced to the West.

"These pathogens just wiped out the native people, who had no immunity to them at all. And we're doing it again. We're doing it this time with toxic ideas."
— Dan Dennett

The definitive vector for the spread of novel memes - the Internet - is now busy shipping ideas globally.

And unlike biological immunity, which is passed on through the genes, each new generation has to *relearn* their memetic immunity.

Culture is learned. It is memetic, not genetic.

This may be its essential, defining feature. Unlike traits that are inherited or skills that are innate, culture has to be transferred to the young via non-biological means.

Whether we become immune to reason or faith (or exhibit a mix of the two) is decided by accident of birth; by the values embedded in the culture we happen to find ourselves in, and through the education we receive.

Wisdom is the facility to sensibly handle memes.

Exposure to a wide spread of ideas, that powerful and perhaps most dangerous of commodities, is like exposure to any pathogen: what doesn't kill you will make you stronger.

"The pen is mightier than the sword."
— Edward Bulwer-Lytton

"Any tool is a weapon if you hold it right."
— Ani DiFranco

burn this book

Unlike the library of Alexandria, you can't burn the Internet.

No longer is it possible, by destroying the vessel, to destroy the content: the content no longer solely resides in the vessel.

The template for a society comes from the ideas a society has - *or is allowed to have* - and because these ideas are transmitted by the media (books, for example) totalitarian ideologies will routinely seek to control or limit them.

What these strictures seek to impose is a *monoculture*, a designed, state-sanctioned society with state-sanctioned values and beliefs.

The justification for this is generally framed as an appeal to social justice, stability and morality. Freedom is the freedom to sink into anarchy, to entertain unapproved ideas. Only by controlling the populace can good be served. People must be saved from themselves.

To codify and promote the correct 'philosophy for living', a state-sanctioned book is usually produced.

A manifesto, a bible.

But being inerrant, these books tend to fall out of step with advances elsewhere, and eventually a gulf opens up between faith and fact. *Education itself* becomes dangerous to the monoculture.

During Pol Pot's genocidal regime which killed nearly two million Cambodians in the 1970s, thousands were murdered for being 'intellectuals' – simply wearing glasses could mean a death sentence.

In 2009, Mohammed Yusuf, leader of Nigeria's *Boko Haram* (translation: 'Western education is a sin') militant Islamist group stated: *"Education is mixed with issues that run contrary to our beliefs . . . like saying the world is a sphere. It runs contrary to the teachings of Allah. We reject it."*

A 2010 report from the United Nations Educational, Scientific and Cultural Organisation warns of a *"significant increase"* in attacks on education. Covering bombings and assassinations on staff and pupils in 31 countries, it opens by describing a 2008 attack on a group of schoolgirls and their teachers in Afghanistan. Opposed to the education of women, the perpetrators threw battery acid in pupils' faces.

"Where they burn books, they will ultimately also burn people."
— Heinrich Heine

Above: In 1933 Nazis burned the works of Jewish
authors and other works considered "un-German".

that'll learn ya

"Education is the most powerful weapon which you can use to change the world."
— Nelson Mandela

When it comes to the question of *why* people believe what they believe, one answer always comes top of the list: "*I was brought up that way*".

"Give me the child for his first seven years, and I will give you the man."
— The 'Jesuit boast'

We are embedded in our cultures. So much so, that the values and beliefs contained in the culture can form the bedrock of our identities. To reassess one's beliefs, sometimes one must be prepared to reassess one's very identity.

"The most absolute authority is that which penetrates into a man's innermost being and concerns itself no less with his will than with his actions."
— Jean-Jacques Rousseau

This is why questioning a deeply held belief can be perceived as a criticism of the believer – and by extension, their very culture, history and values.

After decades of growing secularisation in Western education, the number of 'faith' schools, those that promote a single religious belief system, is for the first time in recent history increasing.

In the US, supporters of 'intelligent design', a rebranded form of biblical 'young-earth' creationism, are campaigning for it to be taught in state science lessons alongside evolution.

"A phrase like 'Catholic child' or 'Muslim child' should clang furious bells of protest in the mind. Children are too young to know their religious opinions. We'd be aghast to be told of a Leninist child or a neo-conservative child or a Hayekian monetarist child. [They are] not 'Christian children' but 'children of Christian parents'."
— Richard Dawkins

The Taliban disapproved of girls aged 10 and over going to school at all.

"The illiterate of the 21st century will not be those who cannot read and write, but those who cannot learn, unlearn, and relearn."
— Alvin Toffler

"Men fear thought as they fear nothing else on earth – more than ruin – more even than death. Thought is subversive and revolutionary, destructive and terrible, thought is merciless to privilege, established institutions, and comfortable habit. Thought looks into the pit of hell and is not afraid. Thought is great and swift and free, the light of the world, and the chief glory of man."
— Bertrand Russell

Above: Emmanuel Church of England Primary School
West Hampstead, London UK

enlighten me

Learning which is transmitted by rote and ceremony is particularly rigid and inimical to rational enquiry, a quality which makes it an extremely efficient meme replicator:

"Religions that preach of the value of faith-based belief over evidence from everyday experience or reason inoculate societies against many of the most basic tools people commonly use to evaluate their ideas."
— Susan Blackmore

The Enlightenment, the period of cultural and philosophical revolution centred on the 18th century, has been defined by Kant in *What is Enlightenment?* (1784) as the *"freedom to use one's own intelligence"*.
It promoted reason as the primary source of legitimate authority.

Enlightenment values of 'rational, critical, and genuinely open discussion' were spread via the explosion of new printed materials: books, pamphlets, newspapers and journals. In other words, the *contemporary media for the transmission of ideas and attitudes.*

An inevitable side effect of this intellectual awakening was a critical questioning of traditional institutions, customs, and mores. As new ideas spread, then as now, the old authorities retrenched.

While Ann Landers, the noted American advice columnist, is quoted as saying that *"No one has the right to destroy another person's belief by demanding empirical evidence"*, Galileo Galilei, someone who had first hand experience of the mismatch of evidence and belief, opined that *"I do not feel obliged to believe that the same God who has endowed us with sense, reason, and intellect has intended us to forgo their use."*

'Natural Philosophy', the study of the 'workings of nature', was what science was called before it was called science. Based on the principles of analysis and observation, later codified as the *experimental method,* it was a *democratisation of enquiry* and a fundamental break from the traditional worldview in which knowledge was passed down by *authority* – via revered institutions, sanctioned texts and initiated elders.

"Reasonable argument is impossible when authority becomes the arbiter."
— Orson Scott Card

In order to understand the world, we must look at the world, not the word.

fictions, facts and the bit between

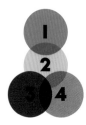

Category 1 – FACTS
Stuff that Is.
Examples: 2+2=4, or dinosaurs are more than 6000 years old.

Category 2 – THEORIES
Stuff that May Be.
Plausible models that are advanced by way of explanation.
Examples: mythology, horoscopes, philosophy, divination, religion, alchemy, unproven ideas in science.

Category 3 – FICTIONS
Stuff we Make Up.
Creative works that, through metaphor, recreation or allusion, may illuminate facts or otherwise offer insights, moral guidance or pleasure.
Examples: storytelling, film, theatre, art, dance, song.

Category 4 – FALSEHOODS
Stuff that Isn't.
Examples: 2+2=5, dinosaurs are less than 6000 years old.

Category 1 facts are true, by definition. They have to be *internally and externally consistent,* that is logical and in agreement with the evidence.

Category 3 fictions are not true in the literal sense (by definition) but through analogy and illustration can offer valuable cultural and moral insights. This category simply has to be *internally self-consistent* to seem convincing.

Some genres of fiction may even be peppered with borrowed facts for verisimilitude – the historical drama, for example.

"Art is a lie to tell the truth."
— Pablo Picasso

Items in Category 2 may be true OR false. Deciding upon which is the business of rational enquiry and the weighing of evidence. However, It is easy to be seduced by their resonance in Category 3, and in so doing let them sneak up to Category 1 status.

Because a certain 'philosophy for living' may hold some very useful personal or moral guidance, and may even be internally self-consistent, this does not guarantee it is true in the first sense - *that is, consistent with the facts.*

category three fictions

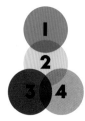

Stories, like theories, need to be self consistent, but unlike theories they ultimately do not need to conform to the objective world to be of value. Within their own frame, self-consistency is all that is required.

Culture has many aspects of a fictional self-consistent construct; that is, of *art.* Unlike bare facts, it is the carrier of *social and moral value;* hence the passion with which it is defended and promoted. It is thus no less important for being a man-made, artificial construct.

Any work – *this book, for example* – once created, has a physical existence in the material world – it *is.* Stories and myths, and the philosophies for living they describe, have their own form of objective reality – in the *memeworld.*

"God exists, if only in the form of a meme with high survival value, or infective power, in the environment provided by human culture."
— Richard Dawkins

Culture is the communal art project of which we all share authorship.

If certain cultural ideas are at variance with Category I facts, this may not be sufficient to undermine them because it misses their primary function – which is not to explain the objective world of nature but the subjective world of *value.* This subjective world made objective is the sphere of culture.

If Category I facts tell us about nature, Category 3 fictions tell us about ourselves.

If art is not *truth,* conversely *facts* do not make *fiction* less resonant.

category one facts

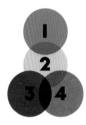

The seductive power of an ideology derives from its narrative and explanatory persuasiveness: its resonance in Categories 2 and 3.

Grounded in culture, it must nevertheless appeal to Category I Fact status to solidify and maintain its position. The stability of a culture and the people who inhabit it can depend crucially on the veracity of the ideology; it can provide a strong identity, cultural continuity, and a set of moral values.

Some ideologies originated long before the decoupling of religion and ethics, myth and history, natural fact and cultural symbolic appropriation. These are the ideologies that have a particular disadvantage in the face of rational thought and observational evidence.

"You are the worst civilization witnessed by the history of mankind. You are the nation who, rather than ruling by the Shariah of Allah in its Constitution and Laws, choose to invent your own laws as you will and desire. You separate religion from your policies, contradicting the pure nature which affirms Absolute Authority to the Lord and your Creator . . . I'm fighting so I can die a martyr and go to heaven to meet Allah."
— Osama bin Laden

"Looking back at the worst times, it always seems that they were times in which there were people who believed with absolute faith and absolute dogmatism in something. And they were so serious in this matter that they insisted that the rest of the world agree with them."
— Richard Feynman

Nature does not care what we suppose it to be - nature just *is,* regardless, and has been before we arrived, and will be long after we have gone. If any ideology finds itself at odds with the facts, however useful and staunchly defended it may be from a moral or cultural perspective, it is only *self-reflective.* The real world may have other ideas.

Proponents of 'ideological phobia', by equating the concept with homophobia or racism, assume that all ideologies, like people, should be judged equal. Humans are, in a secular democracy, equal under the law; *ideas are not.* Though they may live within and be transmitted by people, ideas are not people and so, unlike their hosts, can derive no special privilege.

Ideas don't have rights.

"Our perceptions of the world are corrected by our knowledge."
— Arthur Koestler

N°1

definitions

CULTURE (noun)
Etymology: Middle English, cultivated land, cultivation, from Anglo-French, from Latin *cultura,* from *cultus*
Date: l5th century

l: Cultivation, tillage.

2: The act of developing the intellectual and moral faculties, especially by education.

3a: Enlightenment and excellence of taste acquired by intellectual and aesthetic training **b:** Acquaintance with and taste in fine arts, humanities and broad aspects of science.

4a: The evolved human capacity to classify and represent experiences with symbols, and to act imaginatively and creatively **b:** the integrated pattern of human knowledge, belief, and behavior that depends upon the capacity for learning and transmitting knowledge to succeeding generations **c:** the customary beliefs, social forms, and material traits of a racial, religious, or social group; also the characteristic features of everyday existence (as diversions or a way of life) shared by people in a place or time, eg. 'popular culture' **d:** the set of shared attitudes, values, goals, and practices that characterizes an institution or organization **e:** the set of values, conventions, or social practices associated with a particular field, activity, or societal characteristic.

5: the act or process of cultivating living material (as bacteria or viruses) in prepared nutrient media; also a product of such cultivation.

CULT (noun)
Etymology: French & Latin; French *culte,* from Latin *cultus* care, adoration, from *colere* to cultivate.
Date: l6l7

l: Formal religious veneration: worship.

2: A system of religious beliefs and ritual; also its body of adherents.

3: A religion regarded as unorthodox or spurious; also its body of adherents.

4a: Great devotion to a person, idea, object, movement, or work (as a film or book); especially such devotion regarded as a literary or intellectual fad **b:** the object of such devotion **c:** a usually small group of people characterized by such devotion.

-URE (noun suffix)
Etymology: Middle English, from Anglo-French, from Latin *-ura*

l: Act, process.

2: Office, function; also body performing such a function, eg. 'legislat-*ure*'.

DEFINITION (noun)
Etymology: Middle English *diffinicioun,* from Anglo-French, from Latin *definition-, definitio,* from *definire*
Date: l4th century

l: An act of determining; specifically the formal proclamation of a Roman Catholic dogma.

2a: A statement expressing the essential nature of something **b:** a statement of the meaning of a word or word group or a sign or symbol: 'dictionary definitions' **c:** a product of defining.

3: The action or process of defining.

4a: The action or the power of describing, explaining, or making definite and clear: 'the definition of a telescope', 'her comic genius is beyond definition' **b:** clarity of visual presentation, distinctness of outline or detail, eg. 'improve the definition of an image' **c:** clarity especially of musical sound in reproduction **d:** sharp demarcation of outlines or limits.

Merriam-Webster Dictionary, Wikipedia

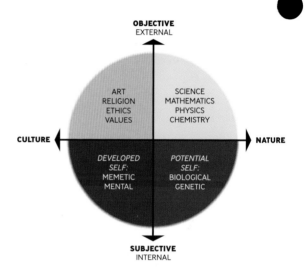

combating science with science

The gun is the favourite means of persuasion for the inarticulate.

"Praise the Lord and pass the ammunition."
— Howell Forgy

Mikhail Kalashnikov's AK47 assault rifle is the insurgent's weapon of choice. Available for $30–$125, one million are manufactured illegally without a licence every year. The AK47 is included in the flag of Mozambique and its coat of arms, the flag of Hezbollah, and the logo of the Iranian Islamic Revolutionary Guards Corps. Most recently they have been seen in the hands of extremist factions in Afghanistan and Iraq.

"Many nations are struggling against modern civilization for the right to worship their ancient gods and obey the ancient divine injunctions. They carry on their struggle using weapons provided by the very civilization they oppose. They employ radar, computers, lasers, nerve gases, and perhaps, in the future, even nuclear weapons – all products of the world of modern civilization. In contrast with these technological inventions, other products of this civilization – like democracy or the idea of human rights – are not accepted in many places in the world because they are deemed to be hostile to local traditions."
— Vaclav Havel

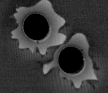

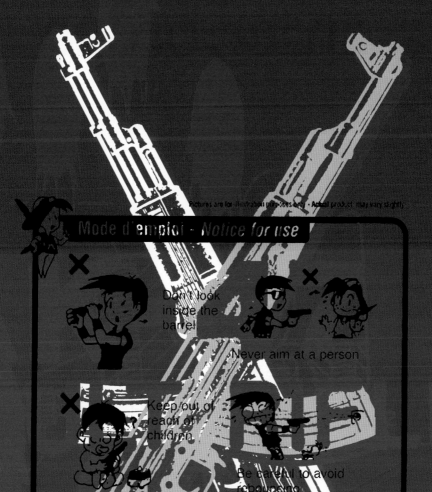

Pictures are for illustration purposes only • Actual product may vary slightly

Mode d'emploi - *Notice for use*

Don't look inside the barrel

Never aim at a person

Keep out of reach of children

Be careful to avoid rebounding

order, order

"So every creative act strives to attain an absolute status; it longs to create a world of beauty to triumph over chaos and convert it to order."
— Rowan D. Williams

"Communism and fascism or Nazism, although poles apart in their intellectual content, are similar in this: that both have emotional appeal to the type of personality that takes pleasure in being submerged in a mass movement and submitting to superior authority."
— James A. C. Brown

"What are the moral convictions most fondly held by barbarous and semi-barbarous people? They are the convictions that authority is the soundest basis of belief; that merit attaches to readiness to believe; that the doubting disposition is a bad one, and skepticism is a sin."
— Thomas Henry Huxley

"Good intentions will always be pleaded for every assumption of authority. It is hardly too strong to say that the Constitution was made to guard the people against the dangers of good intentions. There are men in all ages who mean to govern well, but they mean to govern. They promise to be good masters, but they mean to be masters."
— Daniel Webster

"The welfare of the people in particular has always been the alibi of tyrants, and it provides the further advantage of giving the servants of tyranny a good conscience."
— Albert Camus

"I know no safe depositary of the ultimate powers of the society but the people themselves; and if we think them not enlightened enough to exercise their control with a wholesome discretion, the remedy is not to take it from them, but to inform their discretion by education."
— Thomas Jefferson

"The bourgeoisie is many times stronger than we. To give it the weapon of freedom of the press is to ease the enemy's cause, to help the class enemy. We do not desire to end in suicide, so we will not do this."
— Vladimir Ilyich Lenin

The dictator fears the populace will reduce society to chaos if they're given the opportunity; the democrat fears the dictator will do exactly the same.

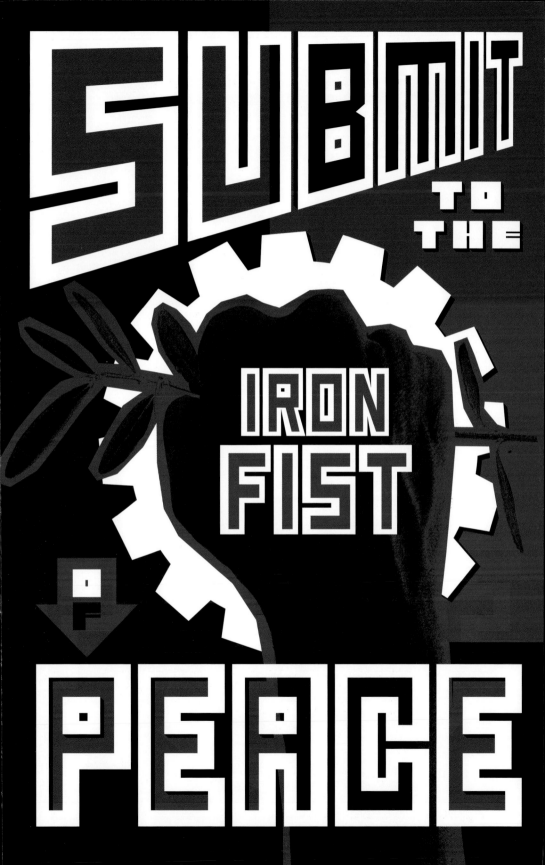

head of ideas

"Human history, in essence, is the history of ideas."
— H. G. Wells

During China's Great Leap Forward, the ruling elite's implementation of novel (but now discredited) agricultural innovations actually *cut* grain production. Despite this, local party leaders reported ever larger harvests, inflating actual figures up to ten times in a race to please their superiors and meet Mao himself.

These reports, used as a basis for the state to calculate grain exports, left barely enough for Chinese workers themselves to live on. When natural disaster struck, the great famine of 1958-1960 – the 'Three Bitter Years' – ensued. Between 14 and 43 million people died of starvation.

"In Xinyang, people starved at the doors of the grain warehouses. As they died, they shouted, 'Communist Party, Chairman Mao, save us'. If the granaries of Henan and Hebei had been opened, no-one need have died. Officials did not think to save them. Their only concern was how to fulfil the delivery of grain."
— Yang Jisheng

Hierarchical cultures and ideologies are especially prone to the 'acolyte error': even without specific encouragement, rational individuals can be induced to behave in ways that they would not normally entertain as they seek favour and position. Even in the face of hard evidence, the accolyte will find it hard to contemplate any thought or action that might undermine a structure in which such a heavy personal investment has been made. Reverence for an idea, or its human figurehead, can be willingly maintained even at great personal sacrifice.

The more steps in the hierarchy, the longer the line of communication and the more distant the decision-maker is from the *effects* of their decisions. Like Chinese whispers, the signal degrades, and without clear feedback from bottom to top an entity, whether ideological, political, corporate, tribal or biological, is more likely to harm itself.

A meme can be so persuasive that often no direct authoritarian top-down encouragement or persuasion is needed to ensure its propagation.

For those who subscribe to a religious worldview, 'leaders' can be so distant as to be completely invisible or inscrutable; for their adherents, jostling for the ultimate reward in the afterlife, any act can become permissible.

"Those who can make us believe absurdities can make us commit atrocities."
— Voltaire

the headless idea

Without an officially appointed memetic chairman, we are free to submit to any idea of our own choosing.

With every flavour easily available via the internet, an infectious idea does not need a pusher, a human salesman or a leader to promote it.

We are swapping vertical bureaucratic signal attenuation for horizontal signal feedback and amplification.

Mobile phone footage and twitter messaging meant that the recent pro-democracy uprisings in Iran were followed globally, that participants could communicate with each other in real time, and were aware how the unfolding drama was progressing around them, independent of state controlled media channels.

"Whoever controls the media, the images, controls the culture."
— Allen Ginsberg

Coming to symbolise this movement was Neda, a 26-year old woman apparently shot by a passing militiaman. Her death, captured in grainy mobile phone footage, instantly became one of the most viewed clips on the internet, a resonant icon of the struggle.

Democracy 2.0. The revolution *will* be televised – on YouTube.

Now that we are so intimately connected to our peers, the memetic central nervous system that is the internet is coming into its own.

Whether dedicated to democracy or terrorism, liberty or tyranny, powerful ideas are travelling further and faster than ever before.

Some of these ideas are so contagious that they are capable of dangerously radicalising individuals, inspiring them to commit horrific acts of terrorism even in the absence of any specific command or direct contact with an ideology's leaders.

"We are now witnessing the emergence of a leaderless movement, consisting of individuals who are self-radicalised and self-recruited."
— Ustaz Mohamed Bin Ali,
Straits Times

For good or ill a virulent meme – *a headless idea* – can recruit an enthusiastic and devoted 'middle management' to its cause.

The meme alone is enough.

The headless idea cannot be beheaded because, like the internet itself, it has no centre, no head to remove – like a chicken with a wrung neck, it retains its own volition.

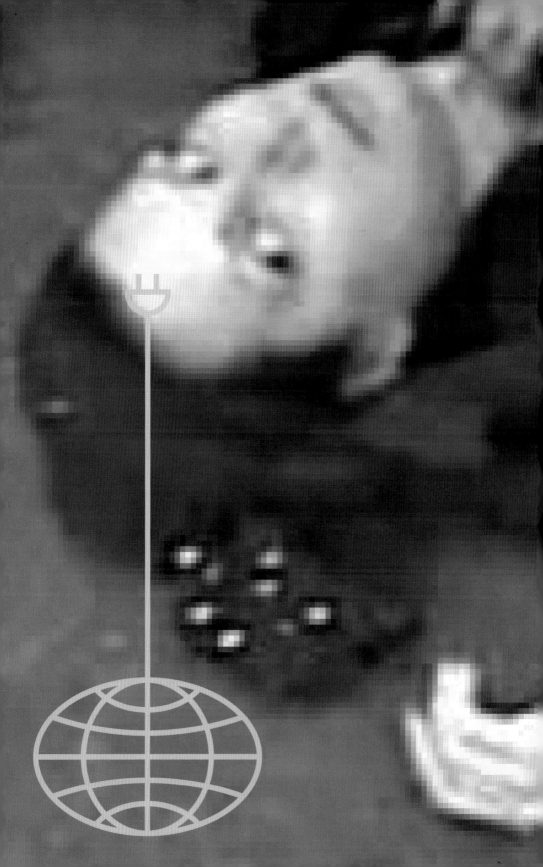

a democracy of ideas

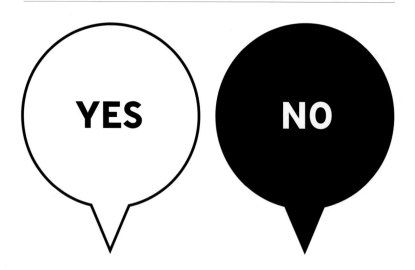

the thin formica veneer of civilisation

Democratisation of culture, like the democratisation of TV, opens up the range of content: along with more of the good, there is more of the bad and much, much more of the indifferent.

Whether this is considered good or bad for culture as a whole is the subject of heated debate.

Either left to its own devices, a more democratic, more 'popular' culture is capable of greatness; or, like the disruptive kid in the classroom, the bully who dominates the proceedings, it will bring everyone down to its own low level.

In fact, as the remit broadens, we move in both directions at once.

A democratised culture begins to reflect the range of opinions and tastes of the people of which it consists rather than those of the political or cultural elite.

Should the state fund opera, for example, an artform unable to support itself unaided? Or should Darwinian natural selection be left to take its course?

More broadly, should our individual choices, moral, cultural or personal, be dictated by an authority, whether that be a religion or the state? To what extent should we be free to make our own judgements?

The dilemma boils down to whether we are considered *capable* of making our own judgements, or need, like those unruly children, to be guided in our adult lives as well as our formative years; whether exposure to certain memes can be helpful or extremely damaging, and therefore we need to be protected from them; whether, at base, Man is naturally 'good', or *"civilization merely a thin veneer"*, which, as J.G. Frazer opined, *"the hard knocks of life soon abrade, exposing the solid core of paganism and savagery below"*.

As the old hierarchies are levelled, will those who simply shout the loudest be the ones whose opinions are heard? Will the playground bully or the powerful and connected simply exploit the weak and powerless?

In the electronic democracy of ideas, it becomes ever more urgent that we develop a sense, not of scepticism or the blind acceptance of authority, but of *independent analysis*. It is precisely those societies that permit their populace the least self expression that fear this bypassing of the traditional hierarchy the most, and maybe for good reason: unaccustomed to plurality, their populations may have seriously underdeveloped memetic defences.

Get streetwise in the global village.

336

Opposite top: Icon seller, Hong Kong
Opposite, bottom: Icon seller, Peru

JUNK CULTURE

With the democratisation and spread of culture comes the spread of *junk culture.* The term is, of course, a slippery one - one person's junk is another's high art.

When George Bernard Shaw's *Pygmalion* was first performed in 1914, special dispensation was needed from the Lord Chamberlain for the use of the word 'bloody' live on stage. People attended purely to revel in the frisson.

Whether material is deemed dangerous or offensive often simply comes down to local cultural norms.

While websites that feature certain extreme content can be said to contravene globally held standards, there is a broad range of opinion - from restrictive to libertarian - with regard to the rest.

In the so-called West, we live in a culture awash with aggressive, persuasive and competing memes, a pluralist, diverse multilayered environment steeped in advertising, sexual imagery, the routine criticism of our leaders and the free discussion of alternate views. So familiar is this environment that we filter it to background noise.

"We have an immunity to all of the junk that lies around the edges of our culture. They're like a mild cold. They're not a big deal for us. But we should recognize that for many people in the world, they are a big deal."
— Dan Dennett

"An idea is not responsible for the people who believe in it."
— Don Marquis

338

dangerous ideas

"The battle for ideas is far more complex than the battle for territory – and likely to last even longer"
— Tim Hewell, *Panorama*, BBCI

In this memetic free-for-all, without an authority to preprocess our information or an overarching ideology to guide us, it becomes ever more crucial that *we ourselves* develop a highly discerning ability to evaluate information. In the internet age, we all have to finally graduate from high school.

If there are certain memes that, like diseases, people in the West may be 'inoculated' against, in a different cultural context they can be considered to be extremely dangerous.

The People's Republic of China, for example, currently has more than sixty internet regulation laws – the 'Great Firewall of China' – that restrict criticism of the ruling party, the discussion of democracy, freedom of speech, or the 1989 Tiananmen Square protests.

On the protests' 20th anniversary, the government decreed that *"In order to improve the internet content and provide a healthy environment for our netizens, we have designated 3 to 6 June as the national server maintenance day. This move is widely supported by the public."*
— South China Morning Post

In response, more than 300 Chinese sites began posting increasingly blasé maintenance messages: *"For reasons which everyone knows, and to suppress our extremely inharmonious thoughts, this site is voluntarily closed for technical maintenance between the 3rd and 6th of June 2009 . . ."*
— Dusanben.com

Other countries censor sites that are critical of the government, contain pornography, political blogs, alternate religious views or advocate women's rights.

Censorship is not only top-down. During the furore over the Danish cartoons of Mohammed, many UK, US and Canadian newspapers decided not to reprint them as part of their news coverage. Whether this was due to sensitivity or fear of reprisals has been hotly debated.

The cartoon itself can be interpreted both as a comment on the dangers of a meme – *fundamentalist religious belief* – and as a dangerous meme in itself – after the image was circulated in the Middle East, over 100 people died in the ensuing violence.

"An idea that is not dangerous is unworthy of being called an idea at all."
— Oscar Wilde

blacked out

redacted text.

blacked out

confidential

blacked out

blacked-out

redacted

the beans out of the bag.

how to kill an idea

Adult

World Trade
Center
Observation
Deck

Memicide - the killing of an idea.

When searching for solutions to many of the problems facing the world today, it is worth remembering that politics and economics are the *expressions* of ideas, not the ideas themselves. Thus, solutions cannot be simply political or economic; they also need to be *memetic.*

Ideological possession can prove very tenacious.

Many regimes, movements, religions and organisations have sought to kill an idea they deem dangerous or subversive, and to promote a sanctioned alternative in its place.

Many methods to achieve this have been tried.

Kill the host.

The problem with this one, as Stalin and Pol Pot found out, is that ideas do not solely reside inside people.

"You can kill a man but you can't kill an idea."
— Medgar Evers

Get in early - brainwash those too young to have built up memetic antibodies.

This one has some mileage. Inculcate, through 'education' at an early age, a distrust of logic, rationality and free enquiry. Promote faith, obedience and conformity to the ideology's tenets. Hitch it to morality, justice and all that is good.

"The meme for blind faith secures its own perpetuation by the simple unconscious expedient of discouraging rational inquiry."
— Richard Dawkins

Destroy the vector through which the idea spreads.

Restricting access to ideas counter to the state- or faith-sponsored party line requires tight control of the media. Where once it was possible to ban books, the internet is fundamentally resistant to such top-down control.

"The way to fight against 'toxic' memes is to also spread 'medicine' memes – like 'only believe proven things'."
— Dan Dennett

The best way to kill an idea is to have a better one.

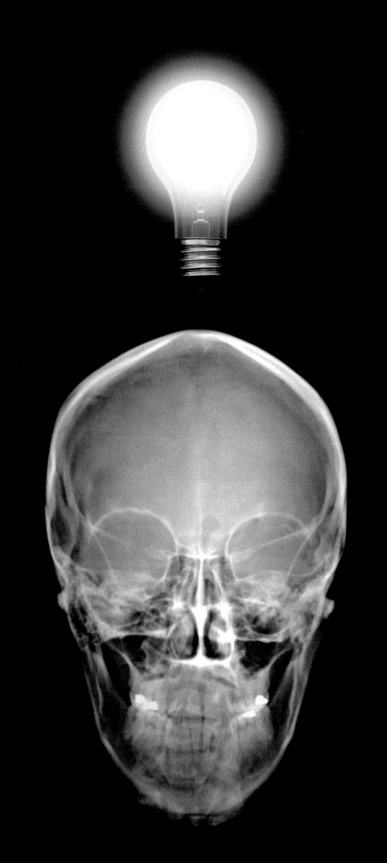

WE INHABIT A WORLD WHERE THE FREE EXCHANGE OF IDEAS IS CHANGING CULTURE GLOBALLY LIKE NEVER BEFORE. ■ IDEOLOGIES HAVE ALWAYS UNDERSTOOD THAT THE REAL FIGHT IS FOR THE INNER LANDSCAPE, NOT THE OUTER, BECAUSE CONTROLLING WHAT PEOPLE THINK IS MORE DIFFICULT AND ULTIMATELY MORE IMPORTANT THAN CONTROLLING THE PHYSICAL TERRITORY. ■ IDEAS GUIDE ACTIONS, AND CULTURE CONSISTS OF IDEAS WRIT LARGE UPON THE WORLD.

DISTRUST ANY IDEOLOGY
THAT DISTRUSTS EDUCATION,
RATIONALITY, INDIVIDUAL
CREATIVE EXPRESSION AND
FREE ENQUIRY. ■ THEY DON'T
WANT YOU TO HAVE IDEAS
ABOVE YOURSELF.

IDEAS
MATTER*

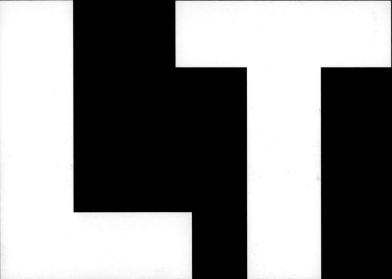

RE

CU

RE

your memetic footprint

" . . . understand, your life amounted to no more than one drop in a limitless ocean! Yet what is an ocean, but a multitude of drops?"
— David Mitchell, Cloud Atlas

Stone-age man would have lived in a mostly if not entirely natural environment. Sustained by the cycle of the seasons, survival depended on reading and predicting Nature's rhythms. Each year was much like the one before, and the one before that. Innovation was measured in ages, and knowledge not passed down orally was forgotten, unrecorded.

We live now in an artificial, man-altered environment. Food and heat are available year round, and the seasons pass almost unnoticed. However, change of a different kind is apace: this year's innovations are building on the last. Knowledge is no longer lost, but is preserved in media: culture has just developed a reliable democratic off-brain memory, and for better or worse natural fact can now stand up to the decrees of traditional authority – if we have the wisdom to tell one from the other.

Our cultural norms are learned through a process of socialisation, education, osmosis, indoctrination and simple practical necessity.

We seek structure.

Is the subjective mind given shape by the objective regularity of the real world? Do we thus structure ourselves in its imitation? If we had no senses, and our entire experience was internalised, would existence have any form or shape, or just be a delirious hallucination?

If it is the very stability of the external world that allows the reflective mind purchase, the more stable and just the *culture*, the more stable and just our interior state of mind – *we* – will be. And vice-versa.

This is the project on which both science and religion, the totalitarian and democratic state, can agree.

Culture is a map that is in flux - absorbing new ideas, new strains of memes, expelling the useless and dangerous, embracing the novel and untried, sometimes mistaking the one for the other. It is populated by reactionaries, revolutionaries, traditionalists and isms in all the shades we are capable of imagining. Society-wide political and cultural movements are our ideas writ large on the culture as a whole, theories applied as grand practical experiment, the population itself its willing or unwilling subjects.

In an electronic democracy of ideas, we ourselves rather than the state or any other overarching belief system ultimately become responsible for our own consumption and production of ideas, for our 'memetic footprint' and its consequences. New ideas can proliferate globally, like an internet virus or a YouTube video, in a very short time; cultural power is devolving to the creative individual.

Soon, we will all have the means to create; we just have to decide whether it be art or bombs.

Culture is our discussion with ourselves as to how we think we should be. It is a map that has the potential for redrawing the territory.

It makes meaningful the set of assumptions, deductions, insights and prejudices we have inherited.

It has a sometimes loose connection to facts, to faith, and to philosophy. It can be impassioned and rational, but also illogical and messy, and needs the sharpest tools in our intellectual toolbox to do it justice.

Because top-down attempts to control and channel it have all ultimately failed, culture is in the final analysis a communal creation, the social and interpretive 'art project' we all participate in.

Culture is the story we spin to tell ourselves who we are.

So who do we want to be?

disclaimers*

*Terms and conditions apply.

*Values may go up as well as down.

*Do not use while operating a motor vehicle or heavy equipment.

*For guide purposes only.

*The management does not accept responsibility for any items lost or stolen.

*Errors and omissions excepted.

*The persons and events in this production are fictitious. No similarity to actual persons is intended or should be inferred.

*Use only in well-ventilated area. Keep away from fire or flame.

*This product is meant for educational purposes only.

*Use at your own risk.

*Some assembly required.

*Apply only to affected area.

*Void where prohibited.

*If condition persists, consult your physician.

*In no event shall the issuer be liable for any incidental, indirect, consequential or special damages of any kind, including, without limitation, those resulting from loss of profit, goodwill, data, information, income, expected savings or business relationships, whether or not advised of the possibility of such damage, arising out of or in connection with the use of this information.

*Decision of judges is final.

*Use only as directed.

*Actual results may differ. For best results, follow the maker's instructions.

*Batteries not included.

*No responsibility is accepted for the use or misuse of any information contained herein.

*May contain nuts.

*Contents may settle during shipment.

*Slippery when wet.

CULT
-URE

This textbook contains material on evolution. Evolution is a theory, not a fact, regarding the origin of living things. This material should be approached with an open mind, studied carefully, and critically considered.

Approved by
Cobb County Board of Education
Thursday, March 28, 2002

For illustration purposes only. Sticker: see Selman v. Cobb County School District. Not shown actual size.

Inspector Knox: So, you see, it was a simple case of mistaken identity.

Ms. Frobisher: But I do still find myself wondering – *who are we?*
I mean, *really?*

LIGHTS DIM, MUSIC FADES.

CURTAIN.

THE END

STOP HERE

PLEASE
REWIND